OPEN TO THE SPIRIT

Inter-Anglican Publishing Network

Australia
Anglican Information Office
St Andrew's House
Sydney Square
Sydney 2000

Canada
Anglican Book Centre
600 Jarvis Street
Toronto, Ontario M4Y 2J6

Ghana
Anglican Press Ltd
PO Box 8
Accra

Kenya
Uzima Press Ltd
PO Box 48127
Nairobi

New Zealand
Genesis
29 Westminster Street
PO Box 22-537
Christchurch

Nigeria
CSS Press
50 Broad Street
PO Box 174
Lagos

Southern and Central Africa
Collins Liturgical Publications
Distributed in
Southern Africa by
Lux Verbi, PO Box 1822
Cape Town 8000

Tanzania
Central Tanganyika Press
PO Box 15
Dodoma

Uganda
Centenary Publishing House
PO Box 2776
Kampala

United Kingdom
Church House Publishing
Church House
Great Smith Street
London SW1P 3NZ

United States of America
Forward Movement Publications
412 Sycamore Street
Cincinnati, Ohio 45202

OPEN TO THE SPIRIT

Anglicans and the Experience of Renewal

A.M. Allchin · Frederick H. Borsch · Colin Craston
Grace Gitari · Michael Harper
Winston N. Ndungane · Donald W.B. Robinson
Vincent Strudwick · Sumio Takatsu · Moses Tay
Gordon S. Wakefield · H.M.D. Westin

Edited by
COLIN CRASTON

Published for the Anglican Consultative Council

Published 1987 for the Anglican Consultative Council
14 Great Peter Street, London SW1P 3NQ

This edition by
Church House Publishing
Church House, Great Smith Street, London SW1P 3NZ
ISBN 0 7151 4761 7

Printed by Orphans Press Ltd., Hereford Road, Leominster, Herefordshire.
Tel. 2460.

Contents

The Contributors

A.M. Allchin is Director, St Theosevia Centre for Christian Spirituality, Oxford, England.

Frederick H. Borsch is Dean of the Chapel, Princeton University, USA

Colin Craston is Vice-Chairman, The Anglican Consultative Council, and Area Dean of Bolton, England

Grace W. Gitari is Chairperson, The Mothers' Union, Diocese of Mount Kenya East

Michael Harper is Executive Director of Sharing of Ministries Abroad, Haywards Heath, England

Winston N. Ndungane is Executive Officer to the Archbishop, Claremont, Cape, Southern Africa

Donald W.B. Robinson is Archbishop of Sydney, Australia

Vincent Strudwick is Director of Education and Training, Diocese of Oxford, England

Sumio Takatsu is Bishop of South Central Brazil

Moses Tay is Bishop of Singapore

Gordon S. Wakefield is Principal, The Queen's College, Birmingham, England

H.M.D. Westin is Cathedral Rector, St Peter's Cathedral, Charlottetown, Prince Edward Island, Canada

Foreword

by the Archbishop of Canterbury

Every Church needs to answer afresh in each generation the question 'What is God doing among us today?' That is at heart the meaning of renewal. As a pilgrim people we must often expect the answer to be uncomfortable. Cherished views or structures will be questioned, and favoured ideas placed in doubt. An attitude of humility and rigorous honesty is therefore essential if we are not to close our minds to those parts of God's message we would prefer not to hear. That is the attitude that I hope will characterise the 1988 Lambeth Conference as we seek to discuss what God is doing among Anglicans today.

One of the great resources Anglicans bring to their internal discussions is an immense variety of traditions of spirituality, theological approaches and cultural contexts. That can be a real strength – but only if we are willing to embark on the hard work of listening to each other and expecting God to speak through those from whom we differ. This volume of essays reflects all the passionate diversity of Anglicanism. In it Anglicans (and a valued Methodist friend) from very different backgrounds speak from the heart about how they believe God is renewing his Church. All readers will find some contributions with which they feel at home, and others that they may find unfamiliar or even unhelpful. I believe that it is the second category to which they should devote most attention.

For many that will involve giving particular heed to the essays relating to the Charismatic Movement. In the eighteenth century the learned and godly Bishop Butler pronounced to John Wesley the apparently judicious opinion that 'pretending to extraordinary revelations and gifts of the Holy Ghost is a very horrid thing'. Now we look back sadly and wonder whether a different response might have enabled Anglicanism to drink the new wine Wesley brought instead of shunning it. We must not repeat the same blindness in our own day. Committed Anglicans have testified that God is doing a new thing in their lives and their churches. That witness should be honoured and assessed prayerfully and constructively. The Roman Catholic writer Ronald Knox in his far from uncritical book *Enthusiasm* gave us the right example when he wrote of the need for disciplined enthusiasm in every Church, 'What men like Wesley and Pascal saw clearly was something true and something valuable ... How nearly we thought we could do without St Francis, without St Ignatius. Men will not live without vision ... If we are content with the humdrum, the second rate, the hand-over-hand, it will not be forgiven us.'

These essays help open up these issues for discussion and set them in a wider context which can only be helpful. They do not provide clear-cut answers, and it is right that they should be published well in advance of the Lambeth Conference to allow ample scope for reflection and response. I hope this will give high place to two characteristics. First, we must be willing to move from academic debate to personal application. In particular, we need to ask whether there are aspects of our church life which are hindering God in his work of renewal. Christian history knows too well the phenomenon of new and exciting movements which become mausoleums. Secondly, we need to remember that renewal does not mean creating a better Church simply for its own sake. At the Lambeth Conference it will be discussed under the heading 'Renewal of the Church in Mission', which implies that turning inwards to look at ourselves should only be a prelude to turning outwards more effectively to the world.

That great ecumenist Visser t'Hooft said that 'all great renewals in the history of the Church have been movements of repentance', and I certainly believe we should read this book with penitence and humility, but also with hope and expectation that in it we see God making his Church more fully what he wants it to be.

ROBERT CANTUAR:

Editorial Note

Since these essays were written two books particularly relevant to the theme 'Renewal of the Church in Mission' have been published. One is *Crossroads Are For Meeting: Essays on the Mission and Common Life of the Church in a Global Society*. It is published by SPCK/USA and distributed in the UK by Grove Books. The joint editors are Professors Philip Turner and Frank Sugeno. As with this collection of essays, the authors come from many different Churches of the Anglican Communion. The project originated in a symposium on the mission of the Church held in September 1984 in Hartford, Connecticut, as part of the celebrations marking the two hundredth anniversary of the consecration of Bishop Samuel Seabury, the first bishop of an Anglican diocese outside the British Isles. The symposium was seen as a way to help the Anglican Communion prepare for the 1988 Lambeth Conference and the book has been designated a Lambeth 88 theme book.

The other book, published by Church House Publishing, London, is *The Good Wine: Spiritual Renewal in the Church of England*, its author being Josephine Bax. In 1981 and 1982 the General Synod of the Church of England debated a report on the Charismatic Movement in that Church, and as part of the follow-up asked its Board for Mission and Unity to keep under review the more general question of spiritual renewal. In its response the Board commissioned Josephine Bax on its behalf to do a year's research and subsequently to write this book. It is her personal account of what she discovered across the spectrum of churchmanship and social background. It would have been a useful piece of study against which the authors of this present series of essays could have reacted in some of the things they wanted to say. In the event only one author, Michael Harper, had access to the book, and that while still at proof stage, and he makes reference to it. While not officially a Lambeth theme book it will be found a valuable aid in preparation for the Conference.

COLIN CRASTON

Acknowledgements

Thanks are due to the following for permission to reproduce copyright material:

The Society for Promoting Christian Knowledge: extracts from the Moscow Agreed Statement and the Dublin Agreed Statement of the Anglican-Orthodox Joint Doctrinal Commission (*Anglican-Orthodox Dialogue: The Dublin Agreed Statement, 1984*).

Word Inc: extracts from *Evangelicals on the Canterbury Trail: Why Evangelicals are attracted to the Liturgical Church*, ed. Robert E. Webber (1985).

1

Preparing the Way
An Introduction to the Debate

Colin Craston

Words, like other aspects of human activity, are subject to fashions. The words Christians use are no exception. But the fact that a word becomes fashionable does not guarantee clarity of understanding or effective communication. A range of meanings may be invested in a particular word, and thus participants in a dialogue can engender confusion by their use of it. Undoubtedly the words 'mission' and 'renewal' are in fashion within the Anglican family. The Lambeth Conference under its Mission and Ministry section is to debate the 'Renewal of the Church in Mission'. None could doubt the rightness of such a concern; but what do the words actually mean?

In a debate in the General Synod of the Church of England on its 1981 Partners in Mission Consultation, the present Archbishop of York suggested a self-denying ordinance: for ten years to be very sparing in the use of the word 'mission', not because of any lack of importance or urgency but because the word could be a substitute for thought rather than a help towards deciding what actually needs to be done.[1] He advocated, rather, the use of specific words like purpose, task, aim, objective, growth, teaching, conversion.

Because of the breadth of concerns capable of inclusion under 'mission', imprecision and considerable confusion have been evident in the past. Like a large portmanteau, anyone might fit into it whatever they wished. Indeed the Lambeth 1978 Report spoke of mission as 'embracing everything the Church is sent into the world to do'.[2] Up to more recent times, however, different traditions tended to make exclusive claims for their own interpretation of the Church's mission in the world. What each put into the portmanteau was intended to fill it, or almost so. For some, mission was confined to

1

conversion of individuals to Christ and their incorporation into the Church. For others mission meant action within and upon the structures of society to eradicate dehumanising conditions and to establish justice and peace in the realisation of God's kingdom; while others, shunning direct political action, saw mission as the expression of Christ's care for the casualties of life. And between the respective traditions there was not much meeting of minds. Then in the mid-1970s, as evidenced by three major initiatives of different origins, a growing consensus became apparent. They were the 'Lausanne Covenant' drawn up by the International Congress on World Evangelism of 1974, the report 'Confessing Christ Today' of the Fifth Assembly of the World Council of Churches in Nairobi in 1975, and the document 'Evangelism in the Modern World' (*Evangelii Nuntiandi*) issued by Pope Paul VI in the same year. In each the comprehensive nature of mission was recognised. It involves 'proclamation, the common life of the Church, and the Church's relation to society as a whole'.[3] Evangelisation, caring service, the common life the Church exhibits as a sign of God's kingdom, and the striving with all people of goodwill for justice and peace so that humankind may more fully find fulfilment – these are now widely acknowledged as the mission in which God calls the Church to work with him. So much is clear gain in understanding and co-operation between Christians. 'There is, however, as yet no consensus as to how each of these aspects of mission is related to the others. Emphasis placed on one or other leads to serious differences of opinion within the Church as to exactly how the mission of the Church ought to be understood,'[4] to quote the Anglican Consultative Council report *Giving Mission its Proper Place*. The Church, therefore, still has exploration and hard debate to pursue, and clearly the task is never finished, inasmuch as the world in which its mission is to be carried on is ever-changing. The reader will recognise in this series of essays differing emphases in the continuing debate.

A CONCERN IN THE FAMILY

The story so far

It is on the word 'renewal' in the heading 'Renewal of the Church in Mission', however, that the major emphasis in these essays is laid. There is, at least, a historical reason for that. At Newcastle in 1981 the ACC, not for the first time, gave consideration to the effects of the Charismatic Movement on the Anglican Communion. Members with first-hand experience shared their knowledge of benefits and problems. While the movement's revitalising impact on congregations and individuals was acknowledged – and testimony to this was given by some present – attention was also directed to its divisiveness and certain dubious theological assertions. There was a general concern, however, to see how the insights of Charismatics and of those outside the movement might be shared for the enrichment of the whole Church. And so it was resolved that the Secretary General should request all member Churches to report on 'the incidence, progress and significance of spiritual renewal, including the Charismatic Movement'.[5] The results were to be studied at ACC-6. The wording of the resolution clearly implied a recognition that renewal might be a wider concern than the Charismatic Movement, indeed might be by other means than that particular manifestation, but that the latter was a way of renewal. The response to the Secretary General's request was too limited to meet ACC-5's objective; only five of the twenty-seven provinces responded, and their statements varied considerably in depth and subject matter. ACC-6, in reviewing the position, no doubt put its finger on the difficulty in its predecessor's resolution when it stated, 'Once "spiritual renewal" is defined with any breadth it becomes renewal of every kind and, since renewal is of the essence of Christianity, the subject really becomes authentic Christianity in all its manifestations.'[6] Nevertheless, the challenge and the problems of the Charismatic Movement could not be ignored. Granted that for some it represented 'the virtual salvation of a moribund church',[7] was it, as some of its adherents claim, the (only) authentic way of renewal, and how did it accord with Anglican doctrine and practice? For instance, how did its emphasis and claims concerning 'a baptism in the Holy Spirit' fit in with traditional teaching on Baptism and Confirmation, even acknowledging that no uniformity of conviction existed among Anglicans anyway? The conclusion reached at ACC-6 was that spiritual renewal was, contrary to ACC-5 thinking, too large a subject to be encompassed in one study, but a study of the Charismatic Movement and its relation to Anglican theology and practice should be undertaken.[8]

When meetings of the ACC are over, the secretariat, guided by the Standing Committee, must pick up the pieces. When the situation was reviewed in the light of preparation for Lambeth – and ACC-6 was in its sections an early stage in that preparation – it became clear that on renewal a problem remained unresolved. Renewal of the Church in Mission was to be part of the Lambeth programme. If, however, within continuing ACC debate and in the Lambeth preparation, study was concentrated entirely on the Charismatic Movement, the inference could be that it alone represented the way of renewal. The Standing Committee had to decide whether the required study, taking the form of a series of essays, should be so limited, or whether the Charismatic way should be included in a wider survey of renewal as seen by different spiritual traditions of Anglicanism. A firm decision for the latter course was taken, thus following the lead given at ACC-5 rather than that of ACC-6.

Recognising our differences

Basic to the Standing Committee's decision outlined above stands a theological judgement about Anglicanism and its spirituality. It will be no small part of the ACC and Lambeth response to these essays to assess the validity of that judgement. It is, expressed simply, that God meets the needs of the Church and all its members with their differing temperaments and cultures in different ways. Moreover, Anglicanism has historically lived out this truth and allowed for it in her various traditions, at any rate in the last two hundred years. Consistent with this comprehensiveness has been a tolerance of new movements or expressions of spirituality within a commitment to Scripture, Tradition and historic order, and its liturgy of Word and Sacrament. Furthermore, diversity in the way God's Spirit deals with people of differing needs and backgrounds in leading them along the pilgrim way of discipleship accords with the evidence of the New Testament writings. Within the Gospels and the Acts and Epistles there are various, but complementary, theological and spiritual responses to the one Gospel, the one Christ-event. The Gospel, as the story *and the interpretation* of what God has done for us in Christ, is a many-splendoured thing. No one standpoint can comprehensively encompass its glory, or completely tell the story.

So this collection of essays has been prepared on the clear assumption that renewal for mission will be seen differently by the various spiritual traditions rightly claiming to be Anglican, including now the Charismatic. Among adherents of the latter spirituality there may be some disappointment with the assumption just described and the decision concerning the nature of the essays. In the

4

light of the experience they claim, it may appear that the rest of Anglicanism is guilty of complacency concerning the spiritual condition of the Church at large, is resisting a holy disturbance of the Spirit and thus is missing out on God's purposes for today and tomorrow. Such a reaction brings Anglicans face to face with crucial questions that ran through previous debates at ACC-5 and ACC-6, and earlier, and at Lambeth 1978. They are: Is what Charismatics have experienced something God intends for all? Are they right in asserting that God is renewing in this age the full range of gifts, vitality and power evident in New Testament times? Indeed, have they understood the New Testament aright?

Listening to one another

The preparation for Lambeth is a family preparation. Members from many cultures and races are being encouraged to prepare their hearts and minds to come together to think, decide, act as a family in which the love of God abounds. It is in that setting and with that motivation the questions and issues concerning spiritual renewal need to be faced. This collection of essays is an attempt to aid the process. Its aim is to stimulate discussion, point up the questions, and possibly indicate some signposts. The reader will hear different members of the world-wide family telling how they see renewal of the Church. The essays are in part descriptive of different traditions of spirituality. Critical theological assessments, however, are not excluded, for serious questions about ways of interpreting Scripture, about the development of theology, and about the discernment of God's will today are involved. But the aim has been to encourage a loving and open conversation between members of a caring family by which all are built up and none is put down. As Christians of different traditions affirm their dependence on the renewing grace of God we hope for greater mutual understanding of spirituality, of what it has meant and how it is to be expressed today, personally and corporately, in a Church committed to Word and Sacrament and seeking to fulfil its mission for Christ.

For reasons which will already be clear a degree of concentration on the Charismatic Movement, its challenge and the questions addressed to it, has been inevitable. Two contributors come from within its own leadership. Michael Harper and Moses Tay describe the movement, seek to relate its characteristics to the experience of Christians in the apostolic age, and react to the question, is this twentieth-century phenomenon *a* way of renewal or *the* way? In response Winston Ndungane looks at the movement from outside, but within a province considerably affected by it. Fred Borsch applies his New Testament scholarship to the interpretation today of those elements in the sacred writings on which Charismatics base their claims.

Turning to other traditions, Malcolm Westin looks at renewal from an Anglo-Catholic viewpoint and Donald Robinson from that of a Conservative Evangelical. While both traditions have experienced the impact of the Charismatic Movement many of their adherents remain on the whole unconvinced, disturbed at some of its manifestations and critical of its theology.

Recognising that many Anglicans cannot see renewal as closely confined within the bounds of the Christian fellowship, or even to church growth by extension, Sumio Takatsu, a Brazilian of Japanese extraction, was asked to write on renewal as affecting the transformation of society for the liberation of human beings from dehumanising structures. If labels must be used this could be described as a radical activist spirituality.

At least half the Christians in the Communion are women. The original intention had been to have several women contributors. In the end just one was possible. Grace Gitari, writing from an African culture traditionally male-dominated, tells how she sees renewal affecting man-woman relationships for the greater freedom in Christ of both.

Down the centuries the religious orders have exercised a unique ministry in the renewal of the Church. Vincent Strudwick describes their role, highlights developments in their contribution today, and indicates insights for the Church at large.

Neither mission nor renewal can properly be viewed within an exclusively Anglican context, even if the bounds of practicability limit one set of essays in preparation for a Lambeth Conference to a mainly Anglican family response. Nor could a responsible appraisal of renewal for mission today restrict perceptions and reflections to the here and now. What has happened in past ages, what has happened and is happening in other Christian traditions, must inform, guide, correct. Gordon Wakefield, a Methodist and a close and valued friend of Anglicans, draws lessons and comparisons from the past while being very conscious of the dangers of nostalgia. Finally Donald Allchin, drawing on a wide experience of other Christian traditions, particularly the Orthodox, writes on freedom and tradition in the life of the Spirit, emphasising the need for personal experience to be set within the treasury of spirituality of the whole Church.

The writers are from North America, Latin America, East and South Africa, East Asia, Australia and England. For some English is not their first language, for one it is his third. Their cultural backgrounds differ considerably. The ACC, and its Standing Committee in particular, are deeply grateful for their contribution to the Lambeth preparations. As editor I would add a personal expression of warm appreciation and thanks for their gracious and understanding co-operation through the whole project.

Many readers will doubtless be able to think of aspects of renewal that ought to have been dealt with, areas of concern omitted, evidences of the Spirit's work unchronicled. Let, then, the debate continue, and, if need be, the literature flow. Only let this plea be heard. Whether in reading these essays, or in subsequent debate within the Communion, may each tradition listen to the others. The rationale behind this book is not to set out a shop window of Anglican spiritualities in which the customer can select according to taste. Rather, the aim is to provide an opportunity for members of the family to learn from one another for the enrichment of all. Mutual challenge, correction, encouragement and sharing of the riches in Christ should be the family objective. 'Let us do all we can to help one another's faith' (Heb. 10.24, Phillips).

RENEWAL OF THE CHURCH: ITS SCOPE AND MEANING FOR MISSION

The Scope of Renewal

Earlier the breadth of meaning that 'mission' may carry was briefly noted. Renewal too embraces a wide area of concerns. If, as Lambeth 1978 saw, mission covers everything the Church is sent into the world to do, renewal must relate to every aspect of the Church's life. One of the major problems for the authors of these essays has been to know where to draw the line. A previous quotation will bear repetition. 'Once "spiritual renewal" is defined with any breadth it becomes renewal of every kind and, since renewal is of the essence of Christianity, the subject really becomes authentic Christianity in all its manifestations.'[9] This twentieth century provides ample illustration of the relevance of renewal to the total life of the Church.

At least from Edinburgh 1910, divided Churches have been challenged by the Holy Spirit towards renewal of the *unity* of the Church. Talk has been endless, progress extremely slow and limited, but the need to be renewed in unity is generally acknowledged. Renewal in *worship* has spread across the Churches. In many parts of the Church renewal in its *ministry* has begun. Leaving aside the controversial issue of women's ordination, which some would claim as an aspect of renewal, there has been a recapture of the New Testament emphasis on the ministry of the whole *laos* and a development of understanding of the ordained ministry's role in enabling the whole Church to minister. Renewal in the Church's understanding of *mission* has already been mentioned. In all these areas excessive and over-confident claims must be avoided; the picture is patchy. But it may fairly be claimed that renewal of the Church *in its understanding of its life and work* has been happening within our century.

If renewal then may apply to all areas of the Church's life, is there any virtue in such narrowing down of the concept as is attempted in these essays? Can we talk profitably about *renewal of the Church in mission?* And if so, what is that renewal? The chapters that follow represent the answers of a number of people, but it may be helpful to set out some basic thoughts to facilitate dialogue.

Renewal in Mission

There can be no doubt that renewal accords with a biblical understanding of God's activity in and on his Church. The God we believe in and follow is one who makes all things new. And that means at least and essentially two things. First, through the New Covenant he has brought in a new creation, a new race of men and women regenerated in Christ, a new order which is the Kingdom, both already here and yet not here, of which the Church is sign, earnest and instrument. And, secondly, the God who calls us is always on the move in history, working out his purposes, which are not totally domesticated within the Church. Those purposes the Church must try to discern with the Spirit's aid and thus shape its mission in the world. As the people of the God of old in the wilderness had to move on when the pillar of fire moved, so the Church is to be a pilgrim people following where he leads. This 'living in tents' way of life is not easily accepted by many Christians. Those who find security in inherited and familiar things are more amenable to settle down and guard the heritage. Without any doubt the

Church has the solemn responsibility of guarding 'the faith once delivered to the saints'. The apostolic tradition, its faith, fellowship, holiness and worship, must be held and handed down. But God's people are to carry it with them in their pilgrimage into ever new and uncharted territory as they try to keep up with him.

While renewal is the work of God by his Spirit, and all our authors whatever their tradition are agreed on that, there must be the response he requires of his people for it to happen. They are to be alive to the Holy Spirit, in living touch and open to his call and promptings, and willing to follow, however uncomfortable the way. Part of Resolution 7 of the Lambeth Conference 1978 'recalled the entire Anglican Communion to a new openness to the power of the Holy Spirit'.[10]

What in practical terms does openness to the Holy Spirit mean – particularly in relation to renewal in mission? Three words may help as signposts: *attention, vision* and *motivation*.

There is need for prayerful and thoughtful *attention* to the situation and changing circumstances in which mission is to be pursued, using all the knowledge and insights that can be laid hold of. The assumption here is that God is at work already, ahead of any initiative of the Church.

Within this attention the eye of faith looks for some *vision* the Spirit may give. The underlying attitude of faith recognises its complete dependence on God, is willing for any possibility, whatever the cost to personal comfort or cherished convictions, and believes the grace and power to respond will be given.

Motivation the Spirit alone can give. 'There is no zeal for mission unless the fellowship of the Holy Spirit is a reality in the Church' said ACC-4.[11]

The call of Isaiah as described in chapter 6 of his prophecy may illustrate these truths. His attention was undoubtedly on the situation in his nation. The throne was vacant, 'the year that King Uzziah died'; after a prosperous reign there was uncertainty. The might of Assyria threatened, but more serious still the people were disobedient to God. In that situation he caught a vision of God in his holiness and saving mercy, secure on his throne. From that vision came the motivation, 'here am I, send me'.

Across the Communion there is a sense that mission is not happening as leaders and ordinary Christians believe their situation demands. The Mission Issues and Strategy Group in its report *Giving*

Mission its Proper Place stated: 'Though there are notable exceptions, the dominant model of the Church within the Anglican Communion is a pastoral one. Emphasis in all aspects of the Church's life tends to be placed on care and nurture rather than proclamation and service.'[12] If mission is neglected, is it not because large numbers of Anglicans, clergy and laity, lack understanding of what mission in their context is, lack any clear vision, and basically lack motivation?

Is renewal, then, a Church experience or a personal experience? Undoubtedly it is the Church that God wills to renew, and any personal renewal of this or that Christian is for the benefit of the Church as a whole and is to be worked out in its fellowship. It may start with some but it must spread. This can be illustrated from the range of 'new things' in the Church this century already referred to, unity, worship, ministry, mission-thinking. In all these areas we may speak of the Holy Spirit as prime mover, but individuals, theologians, biblical scholars, liturgiologists, missiologists, missionary leaders and ordinary Christians, with their minds open to the Holy Spirit and seeking humbly to obey Christ in a changing world, have needed to respond.

SOME QUESTIONS FOR CONSIDERATION

Holiness

Is renewal for mission only a matter of greater effectiveness – more success in making new Christians, or healing the sick and troubled, more efficiency in aiding the hungry and homeless, better progress in changing the unjust structures of society? Or is it also about holiness? There is a long Anglican tradition of those who have emphasised a prior need of renewal in holiness if the Church is to become a more usable agency of the divine purposes. Archbishop Michael Ramsey's writings stand out as an example in modern times. 'You shall be holy, as I am holy', says the Lord to his people. The theme reverberates throughout the scriptures. What holiness means in regard to God we only dimly perceive. Falteringly and hesitantly we use expressions like glory, majesty, perfection, purity, separation from evil, but then, realising the inadequacy of our imagination, fall down and worship. We then recall that this quality of being was manifested in a human life that experienced all the strains and stresses, joys and delights, buffetings and injustices humanity is heir to. So holiness is also a down-to-earth quality of living.

The earliest meaning of holiness as applied to human beings and things is 'set apart', separated for God's use. While completely involved in the world, as Jesus was, the Church is to be, and know itself to be, set apart for a divine purpose. But it is also to become *like* the God for whom it is set apart. The holiness of God is to be reflected in and by the Church – reflected, in the sense that its holiness is real but not its own in origin. A real transformation into God-likeness, as he has revealed himself in Christ, is what the Holy Spirit is given to effect.

In the light of the call to holiness the Church needs to be wary of the subtle appeal of the 'instant' solution to inadequacy and ineffectiveness. Modern technology has conditioned humanity, wherever its benefits are available, to instant solutions – convenience foods, computers, calculators, the list is endless. But there cannot be instant spirituality, short-cuts to godliness, any 'push-button' way to Christ-like character. Moses was forty years in preparation in the desert before God called him to be his agent in redeeming his people from Egypt. What was said of him after that long period could hardly have been said of him before – 'Moses was a humble man, more humble than anyone else on earth' (Num. 12.3). Paul's ministry began with an instant conversion – some things can be instant in the Gospel, forgiveness, justification, a response of faith, a calling – but before his apostolic ministry really began he spent some time, perhaps three years, in isolation in Arabia (Gal. 1.16, 17). It has been said that God's primary concern is with his workman rather than the work. If he gets the workman right the work will follow. Another way of putting it is to say, in the end it is character that counts. Paul would appear to agree; 'those whom God had already chosen he also set apart to become like his Son' (Rom. 8.29). Saints are not made overnight. Christ-like character is not built in one event or experience.

Authority and Authentication

How may what is claimed as renewal be recognised as authentic? By what authority can it be assessed? The significance of the questions may best be seen in a consideration of renewal at the personal level. Undoubtedly renewal must be known in personal experience. As with Isaiah in the Temple court, something has to happen within the personality – conviction, response to God's offer, vision, motivation. But is personal experience the final court of appeal? It is

11

impossible to argue with anyone who takes it as such. 'God has done this for me.' 'The Lord has told me to do this or that.' Are such assertions the last word? Are all personal experiences claimed by Christians self-authenticating? To ask such questions, it must be emphasised, is not in any way to deny that the saving and renewing authority of God must operate in the mind, heart and conscience of the individual. The divine compulsion, whose power is crucified love, must be known and surrendered to within the individual spirit.

The fact remains, however, that human perceptions and judgements are fallible. The human mind has an enormous capacity for self-delusion. We can so easily believe what we want to believe. Deep subconscious needs govern the perception of the phenomena around us, selecting and interpreting to make us best feel secure and fulfilled. Notwithstanding the gift of the Holy Spirit as guide, interpreter of Christ and enabler, the Christian believer needs at all times to remember this fact of human nature. The ancient admonition 'Know thyself' ought always to be in mind. This must involve the capacity to stand back from one's experience and attempt a critical appraisal. The action of distancing from the experience does not involve a lack of faith – the aid of the Holy Spirit should be sought; it is a way of evaluating the experience. In its immediacy and vividness the experience may seem to admit of no misunderstanding. But to experience and never critically reflect is a path to illusion. What *happens* then becomes more important than the *truth*. And the truth to be sought concerns the authenticity of the experience as a renewal given by God's Spirit. In all this exercise of discrimination, however, the individual is not left in isolation. He or she is a member of the whole body of Christ. From first to last, Christian discipleship is a corporate discipleship. What the individual claims to have experienced has to be set within the spiritual wisdom of the Church, and not just the local fellowship or those of like-minded approach, but as widely as possible. If these essays make but a small contribution towards that end they will have served their purpose.

Expectations

What do God's people expect of him in their contemporary situation? Answers differ widely across the Anglican family, and a number of factors underlie the differences. There is the theological spectrum of belief on the nature of God and his relationship to the world. This ranges from near-scepticism on whether God ever really 'intervenes' in the course of human affairs to uncritical assumptions of his manipulation of circumstances, from the trivial to the miraculous, for the benefit of believers, whatever the fate of the rest of mankind. The former attitude may well be taking leave of authentic Christianity, so much in captivity to modern rationalism that it can no longer live with the scandal of particularity centred upon one life sacrificed on a cross outside Jerusalem as God's way of salvation. The latter attitude may owe more to wishful thinking and psychological needs than understanding of God's ways, selecting partially such evidence as appeals.

Another factor that divides is interpretation of biblical evidence. The Anglican faith recognises a primary and normative authority in Scripture. The question every generation must try to answer is, what is God saying today through Scripture? Again there is a spectrum of response, both extremes of which in their different ways show a cavalier treatment. On the one hand, there can be arbitrary selection of Scripture merely to illustrate the most radical of views; on the other a naive, unbalanced wresting of texts from their context to provide direct guidance, 'a word from the Lord', in specific situations. A key question on renewal today, therefore, concerns the use of the New Testament.

A further divisive factor concerns faith and certainty. Faith, for some, affords no absolute certainty, if by that is meant a certitude admitting no possibility of doubt. Faith is seen as essentially the orientating of life in the direction of God's kingdom, a travelling hopefully if sometimes uncertainly on that path, supported by the conviction that God is and God loves. For others, faith lays claim to apparently unshakeable certitudes on a full range of beliefs. Reverent agnosticism is regarded as a weakness. God's ways with man must be fitted into a system, each part of which is to be defended, lest the edifice should crumble.

It may well be that both these positions, as is the way with extremes, are on to a truth, but by over-emphasis and blindness to complementary understandings they end in distortion. Faith is in a real sense a struggle in a bewildering universe, a commitment through darkness as well as light, but it does afford some certainties, of God's forgiveness, of his gift of eternal life, of his calling and grace, of his presence; and so faith even in the darkness is sustained by divine love. A crucial question for faith is, has God spoken and if so what has he said? The question of biblical interpretation thus becomes all-important.

If God has a mission in the world, redeeming and renewing purposes to be worked out, and the Church is called to be his instrument, high expectations would seem justified. Without doubt the Charismatic Movement challenges the Church to raise its expectations. God is alive, he is among his people, we honour his love and power by expecting the mighty works he showed in Jesus and the early days of the Church. So the challenge comes across. Other traditions of spirituality, and particularly churches conscious of ineffectiveness, coldness and aridity, need to face it with honesty and prayer. But, in return, those claiming dramatic evidences of renewal have to be reminded that continuing success is not the only criterion of obedience and faithfulness, whether it is in evangelism, healing or discernment of God's will. Other non-Christian sects, other world religions and political movements sweep in new adherents. Success in healing can foster the assumption that emotional and physical well-being is a divine right for all who believe, whereas some of the greatest saints have been slowly refined in the crucible of suffering. A problem with high expectations is that lack of success at any time is attributed to withdrawal of the Lord's presence or lack of faith. And then the risk of pretence and artificiality occurs in efforts to get back on course. The way of discipleship is nothing if it is not the way of a crucified Master. And, it may be, in following that way some will be called to serve in difficult areas where 'success' in witness and mission is hardly ever known.

The Whole Personality

Must not renewal be expected to touch the whole person, intellect, emotions and will? From Old Testament times the call has been 'to love the Lord with all your heart, with all your soul, with all your mind and with all your strength'. And lest the body be thought of as outside that commitment it is worth recalling Paul's injunction to yield the body as a living sacrifice (Rom. 12.1). Anglican worship may justifiably be claimed to engage the intellect. It stretches the mind and educates in the faith. It can, depending on the way it is offered, also deeply evoke the emotions, though generally under restraint, particularly where a certain reserve still influences worship. For many Anglicans, however, for whatever reason, coldness and aridity have characterised the worship they have encountered, and now in the effects of the Charismatic Movement they find warmth, vibrant meaning and participation. Emotions and bodily expressions find full scope. This can be done at some cost to a full intellectual commitment, notably in respect of songs and sermons.

In an article on 'The Place of Feeling in Religious Awareness'[13] Paul Clifford says, 'Until we realise that all attempts to speak to the intellect which do not grapple with underlying feelings will fail, we shall not make any real progress.' And again, 'By and large, Church leaders have been frightened of facing the emotional basis of religion, lest they should be engulfed in the extravagances which have characterised the revivalist movements ... Whatever its theological deficiencies and uncontrolled enthusiasm, the Charismatic Movement does seem to have rung a bell in the hearts of a host of people to whom traditional churchmanship has made no appeal.'

It need not be a choice of intellectual rigour and integrity or emotional and physical involvement. Both – and commitment of will to obey God – are needed in full-orbed worship. Let an American Roman Catholic Franciscan, however, sum up what he sees as renewal of the personality. 'Through the activity of the Holy Spirit people are led to a personal encounter with God which may be described as a moving experience of God's presence and love, leading to a renewed sharing of the fruits of the Holy Spirit and the highest gift of God – charity, manifested by an effective and affective love for God and neighbour, and a real hunger for praising God.'[14]

Culture and Mission

Emphasis has been laid on renewal as a personal or a church concern. But if renewal for mission is the objective, must not thought be also given to the social context in which mission is to be carried out? Across the Communion a wide variety of cultures shape the lives and responses of the peoples to whom the Church is sent. By way of illustration let us note the following contrasts.

In Sabah the Anglican Church is evangelising, in a race with Muslims, the tribes of the interior whose traditional religion is Animism. Whatever the religion of the headman so is the religion of the village. If he is converted to Christianity the whole village is baptised and then taught the faith. That context can be contrasted with England, a deeply secularised and divided country, where former communities have broken down, and a sense of God largely lost for vast numbers, despite occasional brushes with the Church at times of birth, marriage and death. And even in so small a country, the sub-cultures differ widely, notably between affluent suburbia and deprived inner cities. Contrast, further, the oppressed and marginalised poor of the great cities of Latin America, whose plight is described in one of these essays, and peoples of the Arab nations, fiercely nationalistic and influenced by fundamentalist Islamic sects. Or, again, contrast the context in which North American Anglicans pursue mission with that of the rural dioceses of the African continent, where large numbers are being converted to Christianity, and yet ancient cultural forces, such as tribalism and polygamy, still hold sway. And, can there be any other context in the Communion like that in which the South African Church is called to serve Christ?

Cultural manifestations, however, are not restricted to geographical or national boundaries. Even within the few illustrations given above, philosophical cultures of global range and significance may be identified. Nationalism and racialism are two obvious examples. Another is faith in technology, whose benefits are eagerly seized wherever they become available and by which modern man hopes to manage his world and shape it increasingly to his satisfaction, seeing no further need of the supernatural with its moral imperatives and ideas of divine transcendence and creaturely dependence. Alongside, or perhaps underlying, that faith in technology is post-Enlightenment cynicism towards religion. Scientific rationalism is seen by multitudes to have discredited the authority of religion and consigned it to the realms of outdated superstition, while in the political realm Capitalism and Marxism and their variants compete for control of human affairs.

There can be no doubting the power of the Holy Spirit to convict and convert, however powerfully cultural forces condition the basic attitudes of men and women. Nor must the truth, emphasised by Paul, be forgotten, that it is not by human wisdom that men are saved but by enlightenment of the Spirit as Christ crucified – a foolish idea to the sophisticated – is preached. Nevertheless, within the renewal the Church seeks must be the receiving of divine guidance in knowing how to react to cultures in Christ's name – earlier described as *attention* to the situation. In part, that means understanding how to present the Gospel most effectively in any particular culture. As an illustration we may compare the preaching of Stephen to the Jewish authorities in Acts 7, which Paul presumably heard and which exemplified an approach he himself no doubt followed in preaching to Jews, with Paul's preaching at

Athens in Acts 17. It means knowing what to affirm as true and enriching in any culture, in accordance with the divine purpose of bringing all things into submission to Christ – something the older Churches have often failed to do in planting younger Churches. But it also means challenging error in human thought and attitudes, and out-thinking philosophies opposed to Christ. In its early days the Church had thus to confront the Gnostics, the Stoics and the Epicureans. Whatever the place and impact of 'signs and wonders' in the spread of the faith throughout the Mediterranean world and beyond, the working out of theologies to interpret the Christ-event and to break through the philosophies of the day was evidently a major part of the Holy Spirit's guidance and empowering of the Church in the apostolic age.

These essays are offered with the prayer that the Lord will do what he wills with and through his Church, with all its human differences, and set forward the purposes of his Kingdom.

NOTES

[1] *Report of Proceedings,* General Synod, Vol. 13 No. 1, 1982, CIO Publishing, p. 80.

[2] *The Report of the Lambeth Conference 1978,* CIO Publishing, p. 55.

[3] *Giving Mission its Proper Place,* Report of the Mission Issues and Strategy Advisory Group, ACC 1984, p. 7.

[4] Ibid., p. 7.

[5] *Report of ACC-5,* 1981, p. 54, Resolution 11.

[6] *Bonds of Affection,* Report of ACC-6, 1984, p. 77.

[7] Ibid., p. 78.

[8] Ibid., p. 79.

[9] Ibid., p. 77.

[10] Op. cit., p. 39.

[11] *Report of ACC-4,* 1979, p. 21.

[12] Op. cit., p. 5.

[13] Paul Clifford, 'The Place of Feeling in Religious Awareness', *Canadian Journal of Theology,* Vol. XIV, 1968.

[14] Emmanuel Sullivan, *Can the Pentecostal Movement Renew the Churches?* British Council of Churches, SW/35 1972, p. 2.

2

These Stones Cry Out

Michael Harper

These stones cry out - have always cried
In thousand years of love, grace, power
And of the great consuming fire of God ...

These words rang out in Canterbury Cathedral in July 1978 during the final Eucharist of a pre-Lambeth Conference attended by Anglican leaders from all over the world, including over thirty bishops. The Conference was a significant milestone in the growth of the Charismatic Renewal in the Anglican Communion. Carlo Carretto contrasts 'the great, official solemn Church, replete with ceremony, with visible power ...' with the Church of 'friendship, like the Church of the gospels – just starting, a Church which smells of beginnings'.[1] The Charismatic Renewal smells like this, though like children sometimes gauche and simplistic. Like Pentecostalism it is a movement 'of the people and for the people'. It is a religious force suited to the masses, a new folk religion arising in the ashes of the old which no longer attracts or grips people. When Christian Lalive d'Epinay was commissioned by the World Council of Churches to write a book about the Movement in Chile he called it *The Haven of the Masses*. Nowhere is the Movement more flourishing than in the Third World, where it has probably become the strongest Christian movement amongst the poor since Francis of Assisi.

MANNA FROM HEAVEN?

When God gave manna to his people in the desert they asked him 'what is it?'. Many Anglicans are now asking the same question about this new movement within its world-wide Communion. Is it, like the ancient manna, a gift from heaven, or is it an unfortunate diversion from the main course the Anglican Communion should be on, and a dangerous delusion?

We need to notice the difference between the Pentecostal Movement and the Charismatic Renewal. The Pentecostals are a large and significant series of new Churches throughout the world. They stress the experience of Baptism in the Spirit and the spiritual gifts described by Paul in 1 Corinthians 12. The Charismatic Renewal believes similar things, but has opted to remain within the main-line Churches. This chapter is largely about the latter, although we shall refer to the Pentecostals from time to time.

It is impossible to trace back any great movement, sacred or secular, to one source. Many, however, would say that one of the major starting-points, and the one at which the movement emerged from the shadows, was in 1959. The story begins with John and Joan Baker, an Episcopal couple, members of a church in Southern California. When they visited a Pentecostal church they were baptised in the Spirit. Instead of leaving their church and espousing the cause of the Pentecostals, they brought the fire back into their own church, and witnessed to their rector, Frank Maguire. Nonplussed by what he heard, he turned for advice to his friend Dennis Bennett, the rector of St Mark's Church in fashionable Van Nuys, a suburb of Hollywood. Both these men soon received their own Spirit baptism and spoke in tongues. Dennis Bennett was for several years the main spokesman for the Charismatic Renewal in the Episcopal Church and was to travel all over the world to share his testimony.

In March 1972 Bishop Bill Burnett, then the Bishop of Grahamstown and shortly to become the Archbishop of Cape Town, read three chapters of a book written by the Roman Catholic Edward O'Connor, *The Pentecostal Movement in the Catholic Church*.[2] A few weeks later he preached at a Confirmation on Rom. 5.5, which he had never used before. The next morning he returned to celebrate the Eucharist. He got back to his home about noon. He then did something unusual. Instead of fortifying himself with a gin and tonic he went into his chapel to pray. It was there in prayer that what he had preached about the previous day began to happen to him, and the love of God was poured into his heart. He writes about it, 'it seemed to me like a spring of water welling up to eternal life'. He experienced such power that he was literally pressed to the ground. 'I knew Jesus was giving me his Holy Spirit, and, as I reflected later, this must mean he is risen and present with his people.' Returning to his private chapel after lunch he became for the first time in his life vividly aware of being a son of the Father. Finding words insufficient to express his love for the Father, he began to speak in tongues.

Early the following year, Joshua Ban It Chiu, who was then the Anglican Bishop of Singapore, was attending a Conference in Bangkok organised by CWME (the Commission on World Mission and Evangelism). This body had come into being following the merging of the International Missionary Council and the World Council of Churches. On the day of Epiphany the Bishop wrote in his diary one word – 'filled'. It said it all. The theme of the conference was 'Salvation today'. During his time there he had met Edward Subramani, an Indian Anglican minister from the Fiji Islands. Edward lent the bishop a book by Dennis Bennett called *Nine o'Clock in the Morning,* which described his experience of the Holy Spirit ten years before. So on the day of Epiphany Jesus manifested his glory to the bishop. He was filled with the Holy Spirit, and given spiritual gifts.

Although we have quoted examples of bishops and priests, the Renewal is chiefly a lay movement. It is involving ordinary people, as well as leaders. It is creating what Josephine Bax has called, 'a lay ferment and a management crisis' in the Anglican Communion.[3] Lay people who receive the pentecostal power want to exercise a ministry, but often find the clergy lagging behind, unable to cope with a situation for which they were not trained.

The sheer size and scope of the Charismatic Renewal is constantly being underestimated. Several have confidently prophesied its 'death'. Others see it as a flash in the pan, a short-lived form of ecclesiastical eccentricity. Josephine Bax in her study of Renewal in the Church of England writes, 'some think that the Charismatic Movement as such is over, *but I saw no evidence of this, rather that it is growing ...*'[4] Elsewhere she says that Evangelical Charismatics are the fastest growing constituency in the Church of England today.[5] David Barrett, the editor of the *World Christian Encyclopedia,* has helped more than any other person to chronicle the amazing growth of the various Charismatic Churches in the twentieth century. The Pentecostal Churches have experienced prodigious growth for a Church which has still twenty years to go to celebrate its centenary. There are around 54 million Pentecostal Christians in the world, and their greatest growth is in the Third World. There it has often proved to be 'the haven of the masses'. To these should be added the African indigenous Churches which Barrett estimates to number around 30 million. Charismatics are harder to number, but Barrett has a figure of around 17 million, with about one million Anglicans amongst them, probably the second largest grouping after the Roman Catholics.

The Charismatic Renewal in the Anglican Communion now has its network of Renewal organisations, each one being autonomous, although linked in fellowship with SOMA (Sharing of Ministries Abroad) which was set up after the 1978 Conference in Canterbury.[6] SOMA's Chairman is Bishop Bill Burnett, the former Archbishop of Cape Town; it has twelve International Directors, including two African Archbishops, and I am its International Executive Director.

In terms of church growth and development this should go down as the Pentecostal century. But the rate of expansion is still increasing, and it is likely that the Renewal will grow much more quickly in the more open atmosphere of the Third World. This is already happening, for instance, in Singapore and Tanzania, where SOMA has had significant conferences. Third World leaders are quicker at picking up the importance of what the Holy Spirit is doing in this way; only the comparative slowness of communication in many of these countries is holding up a rising tide which has nowhere near reached its peak.

Lesslie Newbigin was one of the first to recognise and see the importance of the emergence of the Pentecostal Movement in the twentieth century. In his famous book *The Household of God* he describes the Church as divided into three not two streams.[7] He added a Pentecostal dimension to the Catholic and Protestant. But one needs to go a stage further and make an important deduction from this. The Pentecostal Movement is the first new spirituality in the Church since the Reformation which does not owe its origins directly to it. All the other Protestant Churches have their roots in the Reformation and are copies of it; the Pentecostal Movement is an original. This is not to say that Pentecostals are against the Reformation – far from it. They affirm most reformed doctrines, although they tend to be more Arminian even than the Methodists. But Pentecostalism is a radical new spirituality which is meeting the needs of large numbers of people untouched by the traditional Churches, and this accounts for its growth and success. The Charismatics are introducing the same spirituality in their Churches, but in a more culturally acceptable form, and without jettisoning the best of their older forms of spirituality.

What is it that characterises a charismatic parish, or for that matter a charismatic diocese? What makes it different from other churches? What would you expect to find in a church like St Andrew's, Chorleywood, in England, or Truro Episcopal Church in the United States, or a diocese like Singapore?

(1)   A spirit of praise

One of the major contributions of the Charismatic Renewal to the Anglican Communion is its new style and fervency of worship. Charismatics enjoy God. Charismatics worship God with their bodies as well as their hearts and voices. Some of the old hymns expressed this also, for example, 'Now thank we all our God with hearts *and hands* and voices'.

The lifting up of hands in worship, which is commonly practised by Charismatics, is, of course, an old Jewish custom, and was carried over into the early Church. But Charismatics will dance in the Spirit, join hands, sway to the music, shout for joy, and present the Lord with a clap offering, and they will do this for hours on end. It is easy to criticise and accuse such people of emotionalism. But these practices are deeply rooted in the biblical records, and have always accompanied revivals of Christianity. What is wrong with fervency? Should we not be worrying about our easy acceptance of Anglo-Saxon inhibitions – the English way of doing things, which we have exported all over the world? It has no intrinsic value in itself, and when the Spirit breaks through and Anglicans get excited and show it, who can complain?

Charismatics have already contributed thousands of new songs and hymns, and they continue to pour out in what seems an unending stream. Some may be simplistic, even banal; but they are what people like to sing today, and in their very simplicity they are continuing a tradition deeply rooted in the Eastern Orthodox Church.

All this should not surprise us, even if it worries some. When the Holy Spirit came at Pentecost the immediate and spontaneous response of the Church was to worship the Lord with the new languages the Spirit gave. According to Paul 'speaking in tongues' is a form of worship, it is 'speaking to God' (1 Cor. 14.12). Another feature of a charismatic fellowship is singing in tongues, when a whole congregation gets caught up in new songs, with new words, harmonies and descants. It is done spontaneously and can be very beautiful.

(2) *Biblical orthodoxy*

Charismatics love their Bibles. They sometimes deduce weird things from them, but basically they would claim scriptural assent to their beliefs and practices. They love the Gospels, and see them as an accurate account of the charismatic Christ – moving in power, healing the sick, demonstrating the truth of the Gospel with signs and wonders. They see his call to the disciples as one for us today. He is our model and guide. They love the Acts of the Apostles, and believe that we should see the same spontaneous expansion of the Church in our day. It is a book which thrills us, for we see the Holy Spirit doing similar things in our day. The Epistles are so much more exciting when we read them as letters to charismatic churches. We have discovered that, when the Holy Spirit moves in pentecostal power, the same things happen, and the same problems have to be faced. This can be comforting and reassuring.

(3) *Charismatic gifts*

The word charismatic creeps into our conversations more and more these days. Slowly an awareness is growing that the Church ought to be 'charismatic'. In fact Arnold Bittlinger, in a book written for the World Council of Churches, chose the title, *The Church Is Charismatic.* Whether we say 'it is' or 'it ought to be' is a critical question. Certainly one of the goals of the Charismatic Renewal, as its name implies, is to restore to the Churches the charismatic gifts as listed in the New Testament and practised by Jesus Christ and the Church for several hundred years after his death and resurrection. Some gifts are more controversial than others. Certainly it was when Dennis Bennett spoke in tongues, not when he healed the sick, that trouble began. In 1958 there would have been only a handful of Anglicans who spoke in tongues; today there are many thousands who have the gift. The same can be said of the other gifts of the Spirit. For some years divine healing has been practised in Anglican Churches. But the Renewal has added new dimensions to this ministry, particularly in the field of signs and wonders, where gifts are directed more to those outside the Churches than fellow believers. There are today many more Christians developing this ministry as a direct result of the Charismatic Renewal.

But why is this happening today, and why the comparative absence of these gifts for several centuries? There are a number of ways of approaching this question, but there is only space for one. It is now well established that the left and right hemispheres of the brain exercise different functions. The left brain emphasises logic, reason, language, analysis, reading and writing. The right brain emphasises recognition, intuition, rhythm, images, symbols, creativity, synthesis, spontaneity, receptiveness etc. It would seem that in the Western world the left hemisphere has tended to be dominant. We lay greater emphasis on reason than revelation, analysis than synthesis, speaking than listening, activity than passivity. In the East the right hemisphere plays a more important part. We can observe when reading the Old Testament that dreams, visions and the acts of God are prominent in the life of the people of God. The Chinese have for a long time recognised this with their distinction between yang (left) and yin (right).

We can see the same when we compare the Eastern and Western Churches. The East has more of an emphasis on the functions of the right hemisphere, the West on the functions of the left. Charismatic gifts belong more to the right hemisphere, and one reason for their neglect in the West has been the subordination of the right functions of the brain by the left. (It is equally dangerous to allow the right to dominate the left, as Adolf Hitler did.) What we are seeing in the fast-growing Charismatic Renewal is the releasing by the Holy Spirit of important areas of our brain for the edifying of the Church, the overcoming of malevolent spiritual powers, and the reaching of the world for Christ. Karl Barth once said that while the Church could have too little of the Holy Spirit it can never have too much. The gifts of the Spirit are vitally important for the good of the Church. They are offered to every member of the Body of Christ. Just as the sacraments are important for the whole Church, not just Anglo-Catholics, the Bible for all of us, not just Evangelicals, so the gifts of the Spirit are intended for all. Some reject them; others despise them. But they are there as an important part of the whole. In that sense Charismatic Renewal is for all the Church, not merely one of several options.

(4) *Reaching out*

We have already seen that the Pentecostals have been the most successful evangelists of the twentieth century. They have flair, imagination, freedom from institutionalism, firm commitment, vision and confidence for the future. They know where they are going. But in addition they believe in the signs and wonders which, according to the Gospels and Acts, attracted people to the Lord and to the early Christians. They drew a captive audience. People listened because they *saw* the gospel being demonstrated. The more pedestrian, academic and traditional approach of the Church has largely failed to reach such people.

Charismatics are walking in the footsteps of the Pentecostals. They may be making heavier weather of the exercise, and there are reasons for that. Charismatics have not been programmed for the adventure of church growth. Institutionalism still acts as a heavy hand or a brake on fast growth. Anglican middle class culture in the West limits the market they can reach. Charismatic experience does not always release Anglicans from inhibitions which are a barrier to reaching people with the gospel. But as Anglicans are being retrained, as worship is being released, as services become more flexible and attractive to outsiders, as gifts are experienced in services, so Churches are becoming more successful in making disciples.

(5) *Response to a lay ferment*

The laity play a key role in renewal movements. This has never been more true than during the twentieth century, and the Churches' response to this has mainly been creating democratic institutions – giving the vote to the laity. In contrast, within the Renewal, it has been the sharing of the ministry itself which has been paramount. As spiritual power and authority have been conferred on lay people in their thousands, new ministries have been opened up for them. Laity can be even more effective than the ordained ministers when it comes to the gifts of the Holy Spirit. This is why Josephine Bax writes of both a 'lay ferment' and a 'management crisis'. Clergy have not been trained to cope with large numbers of enthusiastic laity clamouring for a share in the ministry of the Church. Most clergy still think of themselves as the ministers. The new scenario calls for management skills for which most Anglican clergy are untrained.

Another problem arises when the church begins to grow beyond its normal size: where is it to grow to? In some countries, like the United States, this growth can be sustained by founding mission or satellite churches in another area. But in the rigid parochial structures of the Church of England this is difficult, as it may mean forming a congregation in someone else's parish. We need to be quite clear: the Holy Spirit, when released in power in any church and allowed to flow freely, will cause that church to grow, sometimes rapidly, with resulting strain on the management skills of the leadership. Many renewed churches have had to develop a new style of leadership, for example new forms of eldership, and these often contrast with and sometimes contradict the democratic forms of leadership developed in the earlier part of this century. The Anglican Church should be sympathetic to these experiments, and should rejoice that many churches, for years in a condition of stagnation, are now growing vigorously.

Where is it all going?

Mark Twain once greeted the premature report of his death as 'greatly exaggerated'. Some have spoken of the demise of the Charismatic Renewal, but it is here to stay. Yet its survival will depend on its ability to adapt to the changing church and world situation, and on its allowing itself to be constantly renewed from within. It has already been through several periods of change, and will no doubt have to face some more.

The first phase of Renewal was highlighted by personal testimonies. The early cry was not 'I believe this' but 'I have experienced this'. The meetings were often a series of testimonies given by people from different backgrounds. One of the most popular songs we sang was 'I don't care what Church you belong to, so long as for Jesus you stand ...' The books we read, the songs we sang, the theology we believed were largely Pentecostal. We had not yet done our own homework.

The second phase I call the 'church phase'. There was suddenly a corporate awareness. 'Community' became a major concern. The body of Christ came into clearer focus. At this point ecumenical relations became distinctly strained. It was the 'wine skins' phase. New wine was looking around for somewhere to ferment in. The unity of the Renewal became strained and in some areas was lost. New Churches began to be formed. History was repeating itself.

But there are signs of a third phase becoming the dominant one in the future, and I have called it the 'global'. The first sign of this for Anglicans was the pre-Lambeth Spiritual Renewal Conference in 1978 and the setting up of SOMA (Sharing of Ministries Abroad) the following year. The Roman Catholics had done the same thing earlier when they held a conference in Rome in 1975 and set up an international office in Brussels, with the support and encouragement of Cardinal Suenens. (The office has since moved to Rome.) A little later the Lutherans set up an international office in Minneapolis.

The fresh vision is now bearing fruit, and one of the expressions of it is large conferences in Europe (ACTS 86 at Birmingham, July 1986), and North America (New Orleans, July 1987). The theme of both these conferences is 'world evangelisation in the power of the Holy Spirit'. So the Charismatic Renewal is nearer to fulfilling its destiny. It has quite rightly begun with the personal and individual – the personal experience of Acts 2.4, the baptism in the Holy Spirit, with accompanying spiritual gifts. It has then turned to the corporate expression of it – finding ways of sharing gifts and ministries together in the Body of Christ. The next logical step has been to look outwards to the world outside and see the command to 'go into all the world' as a divine imperative today.

IS IT THE WAY?

Is Charismatic Renewal *the way* of renewal, or one of several options open to Anglicans? This is an important question to answer. If it is *the way,* we can no longer stand on the touchline and observe what is going on. We should all get involved. Let me hasten to add that in calling it 'Charismatic Renewal' I am not suggesting that it is something to which one pays an annual subscription and joins. It is what the Renewal stands for which is important, and there is no society to join anyway.

To answer our question we have to analyse it carefully. There are three parts to it – renewal itself; the Holy Spirit and the claim of charismatics to a baptism or fullness of the Holy Spirit; and charismatic gifts.

Renewal

Renewal is essentially the work of the Holy Spirit. He is its divine agent. He is the giver of life. So renewal should be an essential part of the regular life of the Church. It is as important for the Church to be renewed as it is for nature. We happen to be in what Brother Roger of Taizé calls 'a springtime in the life of the Christian Church' – in other words, a time of renewal. So renewal is for everyone who has the life of God in them. Renewal is irrelevant only to the dead.

Spiritual renewal will take various forms – sacramental, liturgical, ecumenical, evangelistic, musical etc. One of these forms is charismatic. Like all other forms of renewal it is a part of the total picture. Without it the picture is incomplete.

Baptism or fullness of the Holy Spirit

This is the main affirmation of Pentecostals and Charismatics. It is belief in the recovery of the pentecostal experience of the early Christians. An examination of the New Testament shows that the promise of the Spirit's power is for all God's people, in contrast to the Old Testament dispensation. 'The promise is for you and your children and for all who are far off – for all whom the Lord our God will call' (Acts 2.39). So far as the apostles were concerned there were not two kinds of Christians, some having the power of the Spirit and some not. The promise was to all, men and women, Jews and Greeks, young and old. It has not changed. The pentecostal experience of the Spirit is not *a* way, it is *the* way for all God's people.

Charismatic gifts

What has just been said about the Holy Spirit is also true of the gifts. When writing to the Corinthians, Paul sees all the gifts available to the Body of Christ. No one person has them all, but all have some and are to share them for the common good. The New Testament does not recognise the situation of a non-charismatic Christian. These gifts are not optional for the Church, as if one person can choose the ecumenical way of renewal, another social action and another evangelism. Our ministry may major in one area rather than another, but whatever that may be, three needs are common to all: (1) that Jesus should be Lord of that ministry; (2) that it should be anointed by the Holy Spirit; (3) that it should be endowed with spiritual gifts, whether we be teachers, prophets, evangelists, administrators, healers or musicians.

The Charismatic Renewal is calling on the whole Church to recover an important part of its inheritance in Christ. It is not claiming anything exclusive to itself, as if it had a monopoly of spiritual gifts. They are for the whole Body of Christ, but need to be appropriated by faith.

At the Anglican Consultative Council meeting in Lagos in 1984 (ACC-6) there was a long report on the theme of Mission and Ministry.[8] Admirable though much of this was, there was virtually no mention in it of the Holy Spirit. It reveals a basic flaw in Anglicanism. For example, the report goes straight from the mission of the Son to the mission of the Church without mentioning Pentecost and the mission of the Spirit. Roland Allen knew this flaw and wrote cogently about it. 'The administration of the Spirit is the key of the apostolic work', he wrote in *The Ministry of the Spirit*.[9] The Charismatic Renewal is seeking to put the empowering of the Church for its mission at the top of mission priorities. Without it, mission of any kind is bound to fail.

Josephine Bax, in her book *The Good Wine,* written for the Board for Mission and Unity of the Church of England, urges the Church to invest time, money and commitment in the development of its spiritual life as well as its other major concerns. It is hard to see how, for example, the well-publicised report *Faith in the City* by the Archbishop of Canterbury's Commission on Urban Priority Areas in England, has any future if the Church fails to put alongside it equal concern for the spiritual renewal of the Church. At Lambeth 1988, when the Bishops will be concentrating on the theme 'the Renewal of the Church in Mission', it is vital that the promise of the power of the Holy Spirit be seen as the most crucial factor of mission. Without that power, renewal for mission is an unobtainable goal. Mission without the Holy Spirit becomes mere words. Paul's testimony on his own mission should be ours as well: 'my message and my preaching were not with wise and persuasive words, but with a demonstration of the Spirit's power' (1 Cor. 2.4).

NOTES

[1] *I Sought, I Found: My Experience of God and the Church,* Darton, Longman and Todd.

[2] Ave Maria Press 1971.

[3] *The Good Wine: Spiritual Renewal in the Church of England,* Church House Publishing 1986.

[4] Ibid., p. 46.

[5] Ibid., p. 135.

[6] SOMA, 50 Wivelsfield Road, Haywards Heath, West Sussex, RH16 4EW.

[7] SCM 1953.

[8] Anglican Consultative Council, 1984.

[9] World Dominion Press, p. 42.

3

An Evaluation of Charismatic Renewal within the Church of the Province of Southern Africa

Winston N. Ndungane

'Charismatic Renewal' in the Church of the Province of Southern Africa (CPSA) was a response to a divine initiative. Renewal in the Church has always been the work of God. It is in the nature of God to intervene in the life of a believing community, especially when faith levels drop. God always ensures that life in his Church continues despite people's failure. The story of the new life given to the people of Israel, as articulated in Ezekiel 37, is a good example of how God takes the initiative in bringing back to life a community whose faith had died. The coming of the Holy Spirit upon the early Church was a gracious act of God, which turned people taking fearful steps of faith into bold witnesses. It brought about a close fellowship and a sense of community among believers – to the extent that they 'had everything in common' (Acts 2.44) and even sold their possessions to help those in need.

Whenever God renews his Church, there is vitality and a preparedness for service. Within the CPSA, in areas where renewal has been authentic and deep, there has been evidence of growth and maturity. Through the renewal, as in other ways, God has raised men and women who are willing to serve and to suffer with Christ in a trouble-torn country. It has been our experience in the CPSA that people who are most stable in the renewal are those who are rooted in the liturgy and worship of the Church. In some areas where people's faith has been deepened through the experience of the Holy Spirit, intercessory prayer has become a priority. Some people have had their roots in faith renewed. Consequently, they have been able to handle the discipline and the challenges that have come their way. 'Young' renewed Christians, on the other hand, have tended not to survive the periods of aridity which inevitably come with a mature faith. In times of testing they fall away. This has not been the case where the renewal was accompanied by sound teaching. For the renewal to be effective, it has to reach the very depth of one's being.

However, as with every gift to humanity, the spiritual gifts are open to abuse. St Paul had to deal with Christians who were insensitive and unloving in their exercise of the gifts of the Holy Spirit. Superficial renewal which is self-centred and experience-dominated has come under much criticism. So also has the pietistic and fundamentalist element in the renewal which has been made manifest from time to time. It has so often led to the renewal being viewed as a way of escaping the real issues of life by those who are concerned for social justice and, in particular, by those who are at the receiving end of the Apartheid system.

SOME POSITIVE ASPECTS OF THE RENEWAL

There has been a rediscovery of a spirit of brotherhood amongst clergy who have experienced renewal. Many have found a new dimension of faith and have become effective leaders of vibrant and growing parishes.

Within the charismatic renewal movement much emphasis is laid on the gifts of the Holy Spirit, which are given by God not only to the clergy but also to the laity, i.e. to the whole body of Christ. This has led to a greater lay participation in the life of the Church. Lay people who have become aware of their gifts, and where they are allowed to exercise them, have become in most instances more committed to service in the Church and even more confident of their worth in the sight of God.

In parishes where some people have had a renewal experience there has been much interest in the study of the Bible. Consequently house church groups for Bible study and fellowship have become part of the life of such parishes. Such small intimate groups have created opportunites for Christians to share their lives with one another, to support one another and to bear one another's burdens at some depth in a way which is reminiscent of the sharing of the early Church as reflected in the Book of Acts.

The charismatic renewal has called for a careful consideration of the practice of Baptism. It has pointed to the inadequacy in the preparation for, as well as teaching about, Baptism. While challenging accepted practices of the Church concerning Baptism and Confirmation, the renewal has nonetheless in most cases not overthrown them.

The style in which Pentecostal churches express their relationship with God and the degree of lay involvement in worship and ministry have had much influence in the charismatic renewal. They have resulted in forms of worship, which often include choruses accompanied by clapping and dancing, which for some people have been a source of spiritual uplift.

The charismatic renewal brought with it an emphasis that all that we are and possess comes from God. A response to this has been increased dedication in financial giving as well as a readiness to be available for service in the Church. This was a result of sound teaching on stewardship, an aspect which had been sadly neglected in the CPSA.

SOME NEGATIVE COMMENTS

Generally one of the major negative effects of the charismatic renewal is its failure to address itself to the need for the renewal of the human community, particularly as regards the breaking down of structural sin in South Africa's Apartheid society. Its emphasis on individual and personal salvation has made it impossible for people in the renewal to be involved in issues concerning social justice. This brand of spirituality has been considered by many to be irrelevant for present-day South Africa.

Division within congregations has been another negative feature of the renewal movement. The rift has often been caused by those with an attitude of 'we have arrived'. It is very common for a zealous newly-baptised-in-the-Holy Spirit Christian to insist that faithful members of the congregation must have the same experience he or she has had, and this usually causes resentment.

The increased participation of lay people in the ministry of the Church can lead to problems with authority, and can result in a group breaking away from the congregation into schism.

Some lay people become so caught up in the experiential side of worship that they become 'spiritual butterflies', flitting from one congregation to the next in search of a better spiritual experience. A specific form of this self-centredness finds expression in a lack of concern for the sufferings of fellow Christians.

OBSERVATIONS

Community

The renewal brought with it a rediscovery of the community aspect of our lives. In parishes where a significant number of people have had a renewal experience there has been evidence of closeness and supportiveness of one another within the congregation and family life. As the breakdown of society escalates within our country, the need for close and supportive fellowship within the Church increases. The Holy Spirit gives Christians the self-sacrificing love which makes them able to give up their privileges and possessions for the sake of brothers and sisters in need. The lessons learned about community from the charismatic renewal, if put into practice now, will prepare Christians to persevere amidst hardships ahead, with the security of Christian support.

Leadership

History has shown that, during troubled times such as these, church leaders are prime targets for arrest. An organisation without leadership is crippled. Through the charismatic renewal God has been preparing us for the present crisis, for he has reminded the Church of the value of lay involvement. A Church in which effective lay leadership operates can continue without its priest, should he be imprisoned.

Praise

The charismatic renewal, with its emphasis upon praising God in all circumstances, has provided the Church with an effective instrument for the restoration of relationship with God which has the effect of turning people away from fear and despondency. Community praise has the effect of lifting the spirit and turning the eyes of the Christian community back upon God from whom their help comes.

Baptism

The phrase 'Baptism in the Spirit', frequently used to describe the renewal experience, has in the South African context been unhelpful.

It has over-emphasised the individual and spiritual aspect of Christian Baptism to the extent of failing to assist Christians to integrate life in Christ with life in society. It has also distorted the true meaning of Baptism through the practice of rebaptism, which has taken place in some instances. Yet the Church, especially in South Africa, needs a deeper understanding of Baptism and a more lively experience of all that it means for us. This must include a theology which gives far more recognition to the living presence of the Holy Spirit in the Church. This is because proclaiming God's justice and witness to the Gospel of Jesus by word and deed in South Africa often brings about suffering, rejection, imprisonment and even death.

All Baptism is Baptism into Jesus' death and resurrection. It is a dying and a rising with Christ, as Paul puts it. It is being crucified with Christ and being made alive for God. It is incorporation into the life of suffering. For Christians in South Africa this understanding equips them for relevant Christian witness in resisting the evil of Apartheid and working for a just society. It enables them to see sin in all its manifestations. Christians who experience Baptism in this way also know the assurance of victory over sin in all its forms and the hope of resurrection from all situations of death. This is new life in Christ.

Ministry of the laity

The Church needs to rediscover its true nature and its role in society. The Church is a community of men and women, lay and ordained, who have been endowed with a variety of gifts for service in the world. In Eph. 4.11 St Paul makes it clear that God gives different gifts to various people to equip them 'for the work of ministry, for the building up of the body of Christ'.

It has been noted earlier that the charismatic renewal brought an awareness of the gifts of the Holy Spirit that God has given to all his people both lay and ordained. These gifts are given, however, not for self-edification or boasting. In accordance with God's purposes these gifts are to be shared in the service of humanity. This not only entails a need for cross-fertilisation of ideas among the people of God; it also brings about an awareness of the interdependence of human beings and therefore an obligation to co-operate with one another in the promotion of the common good in the service of society.

Openness to God

An openness to God and the movement of the Holy Spirit are essential elements in the process of renewal in the Church. While the Church has to remain faithful to the history, tradition and kerygma that have been handed down to successive generations of Christians, nevertheless she has to be open to the future as the Holy Spirit unfolds it, bringing the new from the old, leading us into new experiences of truth. The Church ought not to be fearful of acknowledging that she is on a pilgrimage in this world in which there is a continuous revelation of God's activity. In South Africa the Church is called to be pointing to the truth of God's concern for justice and his presence among the poor, the oppressed and the marginalised.

There are some people in the renewal who are disillusioned with the renewal as they have observed it. In their perception the spectacular signs, wonders and activities which accompanied the initial phase of renewal have become less common. 'Things are no longer the same', they say. While it is true that the miraculous plays an important role within the believing community, yet it is not a substitute for faith. It ought not to provide a short cut for full engagement with the challenges facing the Church. In the words of Jesus: 'Blessed are those who have not seen and yet believe' (John 20.20). He himself discouraged those who demanded miraculous signs from him, while refusing to obey his teaching (Matt. 12.38-42). St Paul requested God three times to remove a thorn in the flesh which was a hindrance in his ministry, but this was refused: 'My grace is sufficient for you, for my power is made perfect in weakness' (2 Cor. 12.9).

At times God intervenes in a special and unique way with signs and wonders in order to awaken faith and to summon people to obedient action. The incarnation was such an intervention. While being miraculous, it was God's direct physical and historical engagement in human affairs. Speaking about the incarnation, Frank Chikane, General Secretary of The Institute for Contextual Theology, says: 'It was a revolutionary event ... a liberating action, transforming society ... from which Christians learn that God is not the God who could watch people suffer ... while accepting worship and praise'. The prophet Isaiah put it this way: 'What to me is the multitude of your sacrifices? I have had enough of burnt offerings. I do not delight in the blood of bulls. When you appear before me, who requires of you this trampling of my courts? Bring no more vain offerings; incense is an abomination to me. New moon and sabbath and solemn assembly I cannot endure. When you spread forth your hands, I will hide my eyes from you; though you make many prayers, I will not listen; your hands are full of blood. Wash yourselves; make yourselves clean; cease to do evil, learn to do good; seek justice, correct oppression; defend the fatherless, plead for the widow' (Isa. 1.12-17).

CONCLUSION

Renewal in the CPSA has shaken our complacency and has helped us to rediscover the significance of the Holy Spirit in the Church. Where renewal has been genuine, there has come about a deepened spirituality, a mature faith and an equipping for service as God's instruments for the urgent and pressing task of bringing about God's justice in a polarised South Africa. The renewal holds both the possibility and the power for equipping the Church for authentic Christian witness and the ministry of reconciliation in a strife-torn and divided South Africa. A Church that is truly renewed is one which is a source of renewal within the community. It is our hope and prayer that God will continue to enable us to experience his life-giving power in this situation of death and destruction and mould us into a sign of hope.

4

The Charismatic Movement: A Way or The Way of Renewal?

Moses Tay

Dare the Charismatics claim the monopoly of truth concerning renewal, so that theirs is not just *a* way but *the* way of renewal? Certainly not. But if theirs is a fairly sure way of renewal, then the Charismatic Movement is worth another assessment.

The Charismatics prefer to regard themselves simply as 'in the renewal', but, in this book of essays, they must continue to wear the label of 'Charismatic Movement' since the word 'renewal' has been used by other people to mean different things. Yet the issue in question is whether the Charismatic Movement is *a* way or *the* way of renewal, a concertina term which has been stretched to include many forms of changes. If different things are allowed to go under the term 'renewal' then it is unlikely, on the basis of logic or probability, that the Charismatic Movement is more than *a* way.

For the examination of the Charismatic Movement to be useful, we need to confine 'renewal' to the meaning of spiritual renewal – a discovery or recovery of our spiritual heritage and experience. In practical terms, it means a life-transforming experience of the triune God, such as Isaiah received of God Almighty (Isaiah 6), as the doubting Thomas did of the risen Christ (John 20.28), and as the disciples did of the Holy Spirit at Pentecost (Acts 2). In general the Charismatic Movement is not different from authentic Christianity but its emphasis is on the gifts and power of the Holy Spirit.

It is also important to recognise that renewal, like any change, should be regarded as a means to an end, not just an end in itself. We may like to have a change or renewal, but this must lead us to the real goals or spiritual objectives. In short, spiritual renewal must lead us to fulfil the purpose which our Lord has for the Church and to the manifestation of the glory of God in our midst.

Lord Coggan has upheld what he said at the Renewal Conference at Canterbury in 1978: 'I wish the Charismatic Movement will die, for every Christian should be charismatic.' We share his view. Although this dying Charismatic Movement is increasingly difficult to define, the essentials of the Charismatic experience must be defined.

ESSENTIALS OF THE CHARISMATIC EXPERIENCE

Central to the Charismatic experience is the baptism in the Holy Spirit. It is necessary that we define the terms we use, since almost every term has been used in different ways and given different meanings. In this essay the term 'baptism in the Holy Spirit' is understood to be synonymous with the Pentecost experience of Acts 2. Though the noun-form baptism in the Holy Spirit is not used in the New Testament, the verb-form baptised with the Holy Spirit is consistently used to refer to the Pentecost experience for which the disciples had to wait. This was prophesied by John the Baptist at the river Jordan and recorded by all four Gospel writers: 'He will baptise you with the Holy Spirit and with fire' (Matt 3.11; Luke 3.16 cf Mark 1.8; John 1.33). This was reaffirmed and promised by our risen Lord in Acts 1.4-5.

> And while staying with them he charged them not to depart from Jerusalem, but to wait for the promise of the Father, which he said, 'you heard from me, for John baptized with water, but before many days you shall be baptized with the Holy Spirit'.

That the baptism in the Holy Spirit meant the Pentecost experience was the clear understanding of the disciples when Peter referred to the experience of Cornelius (Acts 10) as fulfilment of the prophecy of John the Baptist and the words of our Lord: 'And I remembered the word of the Lord, how he said, "John baptized with water but you shall be baptized with the Holy Spirit"' (Acts 11.16).

The only other New Testament reference that could refer to the same experience is 1 Cor. 12.13: 'For by one Spirit we were all baptized into one body – Jews or Greeks, slaves or free – and all were made to drink of one Spirit.' This verse has been much debated by scholars and theologians but quite obviously it includes a broader scope than the Pentecost experience or regeneration (new birth). The meaning of this verse cannot be limited in order that it may be used to support a particular theological viewpoint, since it is so loaded with symbolic, spiritual and sacramental significance which we need not unpack. Suffice it to say that Pauline use of 'baptised into one body' in 1 Cor. 12.13 without the specific clause 'baptised with the Holy Spirit' cannot rule out our use of 'baptised with the Holy Spirit' for the Pentecost experience, which is the usage in all the other references.

What then constitutes the Pentecost experience? Luke records for us five such events in Acts 2.1-13; 8.14-19; 10.44-48; 19.1-7; and, possibly, 9.17-18. While the circumstances and experiences were all different, it is clear that the Pentecost experience was consistently accompanied by visible manifestations of the power of the Holy Spirit. In Acts 2, there was the waiting and the expectation at the upper room and the Pentecost experience was accompanied by the sound of rushing wind, tongues of fire and speaking in tongues (languages), and followed by powerful preaching of the word. In Acts 8.14-19 the Holy Spirit was given through the laying on of hands after water baptism. While the accompanying manifestations were not described, it is clear that manifestation of the power of the Holy Spirit was evident, for Simon wanted to buy such power with money. In Acts 10.44-48 there was no laying on of hands; the out-pouring of the Holy Spirit on the Gentiles with speaking in tongues was a surprise to Peter and his companion Jews and it took place before water baptism. In Acts 19.1-7, almost thirty years later, Paul expected the Pentecost experience to be the normative experience of believers. In this instance, the Pentecost experience followed water baptism in the name of Jesus as Paul laid hands on them and they spoke with tongues and prophesied. In Acts 9.17-18 Paul's own experience of the Holy Spirit was through the laying on of hands and accompanied by healing of his blindness and followed by water baptism. It should be noted that in three of the five instances speaking in tongues was clearly described (Acts 2.4, 6ff; 10.46; 19.6).

By and large, authentic charismatic experiences correspond to those described in Acts summarised above. The extensiveness of the Pentecost experience throughout the world both within and outside the Anglican Communion is captured by W. J. Hollenweger's book *The Pentecostals,*[1] and the three-volume documents *Presence, Power, Praise,* edited by Kilian McDonnell.[2] No theology can deny the existence of the Pentecost experience of millions today, neither can it invalidate the reality of such experience. Yet the Pentecost experience is consistent with biblical theology, bringing into life and reality what we have affirmed in our theology and creeds. It seems that Christian leaders down the ages have been slow in keeping up with what God had done, for example Thomas's late recognition of the fact of the resurrection and Peter's slowness to recognise God's grace to the Gentiles. But they did come to terms with the work of God and glorified God, saying, 'Then to the Gentiles also God has granted repentance unto life' (Acts 11.18). Herein lies the key to ful- filling the mission of the Church.

Other common features of the Pentecost experience include the joy and excitement of the reality of God, praise and worship, the centrality of Christ, a fresh recognition of the authority and truth of his Word and a hunger for the Word. Consequences of the Charismatic experience include a new freedom in worship, exercise of the gifts of the Holy Spirit in building up the Body of Christ and in evangelism, the preaching of the word accompanied by healing and deliverance, and the participation of lay people in the ministry. There is often a transformation of community life resulting in formation of communities or home groups for sharing things in common, for renewal and mission. In Singapore a systematic and extensive training of the lay people for lay ministry and the develop- ment of home cell groups for edification and evangelism are our current priorities.

It is important to distinguish the essentials of the Charismatic experience and the beneficial consequences from the non-essential accompaniments which often put off people, for example, the degree of noise, a 'holier than thou' attitude, gullibility, sensationalism, personal idiosyncrasies including bodily postures and actions, and many other forms of 'charismatism'. The caution for us is that we do not throw out the baby with the bath-water.

We now go on to consider some common problems in relation to the baptism in the Holy Spirit.

PROBLEMS REGARDING BAPTISM OF THE HOLY SPIRIT

Firstly, there is the problem of what some call the 'second experience'. On the basis of 1 Cor. 12.13 it is claimed that every Christian is baptised with the Holy Spirit and so it is difficult to accept that he should be baptised in the Holy Spirit a second time or that the baptism in the Holy Spirit is a separate experience from regeneration. In his book *Joy Unspeakable* D. Martyn Lloyd-Jones[3] argues on grammatical grounds that 1 Cor. 12.13 need not refer to baptism in the Holy Spirit at all. In dealing with the issues dividing the Corinthian Church Paul was reminding them that the Holy Spirit who imparts different gifts is the same Spirit who incorporates the believer into the Body of Christ. Obviously, the word 'baptised' in 1 Cor. 12.13 is used in a sense different from that in Matt. 3.11; Mark 1.8; John 1.33; Luke 3.16; Acts 1.5, 11.16.

It is clear that when someone repents and receives Christ he is born of the Holy Spirit (John 3.5-8), has the witness of the Holy Spirit in him and cries, 'Abba Father!' (Rom. 8.15-16; Gal. 4.6). Indeed, 'Any one who does not have the Spirit of Christ does not belong to him' (Rom. 8.9b). Yet it was to God's children (who, by definition, already had the Holy Spirit) that our Lord promised the Holy Spirit to those who ask him (Luke 11.13). Furthermore, we have Jesus who was conceived by the Holy Spirit (i.e. in terms of medical genetics the Holy Spirit seemed to constitute part of his being) and yet the Holy Spirit descended on him from above in the form of a dove at his baptism at the river Jordan thirty years later.

It may be helpful if we take a more human example and ask a nonsense question – nonsense from the other side of eternity. When was Peter converted, 'saved', 'born again'? Or when did he have his 'first experience'? Was it at the miraculous fishing experience when he said, 'Depart from me, for I am a sinful man, O Lord' (Luke 5.8)? Was it at Caesarea Philippi when he confessed, 'You are the Christ, the Son of the living God' (Matt. 16.16)? Was it when the risen Lord appeared to the disciples and breathed on them the Holy Spirit (John 20.22)? Was it when Peter was challenged and restored (John 21.15-18) after his triple denial of Christ? If we find it difficult or impossible to label the Pentecost experience as his 'first experience', especially in view of John 20.22, it is equally futile to try to evade the issue of the 'second experience' by labelling it as unique. Every Pentecost experience is unique to each person but the same experience has been repeated not only in the book of Acts but millions of times today, even in our Anglican Communion. But the so-called 'second experience' need not always be separated from the 'first experience'. On the day of Pentecost, Peter appealed to his hearers to repent, be baptised and receive the gift of the Holy Spirit, 'for this promise is to you and your children' (Acts 2.38-39). Indeed we have seen many receive the baptism of the Holy Spirit at conversion. But where the 'second experience' has not accompanied the 'first experience' due to defective teaching, ignorance, fear, pride or other reasons, it is better to come to the Lord in humility and receive his wonderful gifts than to write off the Pentecost experience on theological grounds. If we have no problem with many fillings of the Holy Spirit, then we should not have any difficulty in accepting a 'second experience' which happens to be called 'baptism in the Holy Spirit'. The analogy of the early and latter rain (Joel 2.23) may help to illustrate further:

	EARLY RAIN	LATTER RAIN
PHYSICAL REALM	Softens soil for germination of grain	Ripens grain for harvest
SPIRITUAL REALM	Regeneration by Holy Spirit = 'born of the Spirit'	Empowering by Holy Spirit for effective service

Secondly, there are some who hold firmly to the Reformed theology of *sola gratia, sola scriptura* and *sola fides,* and yet see the Pentecost experience only for the first generation apostles or the early Church. They believe that the Pentecost experience (i.e. the gifts and power of the Holy Spirit) was necessary for the founding of the Church and before the completion of the Canon of the New Testament. 1 Cor. 13.10, 'but when the perfect comes, the imperfect will pass away', is often cited in support of the dispensational theory, because 'the perfect' is taken to mean the completion of the Canon and 'the imperfect' to refer to the charismatic gifts which have now ceased. This is untenable since the context of 1 Cor. 13 and the words of 1 Cor. 13.12 'then we shall see him face to face' cannot refer to the completion of the Canon but the second coming of Christ. Furthermore the dispensational theory is not based on Scripture, for if Peter saw the Pentecost experience as the fulfilment of Scripture for the last days when he quoted prophet Joel: 'and in the last days ... I will pour out my Spirit upon all flesh' (Acts 2.17-21; cf. Joel 2.28-32), we who are living in the last of the last days must expect to see more of the outpouring of the Holy Spirit, as we indeed are seeing today. If the early Church needed the gifts and power of the Holy Spirit when the apostles could well stand up publicly and proclaim that Jesus was alive, and none could produce the dead body of Jesus or contradict the eloquent testimony of the empty tomb, how much more does the Church today need the power of the Holy Spirit, especially when we are nearly two thousand years from the event. If the view that the Pentecost experience was only for the early Church was a conclusion based on the absence of the manifestations of the power of the Holy Spirit, then this view needs thorough revision today. We must return to Scripture, sound logic and reality.

Thirdly, there are some who confuse the fruit with the gifts of the Holy Spirit, preferring the former to the latter as if these are options. The following table makes clear the distinction and the relation between the fruit and the gifts of the Holy Spirit.

	FRUIT OF THE SPIRIT	GIFTS OF THE SPIRIT
SCRIPTURE	Gal. 5.22-23	1 Cor. 12.7-11
DESCRIP-TION	Love Joy Peace Patience Kindness Goodness Faithfulness Gentleness Self-control	Utterance of wisdom Utterance of knowledge Faith Gifts of healing Working of miracles Prophecy Discerning of spirits Tongues Interpretation of tongues
FUNCTION	For Christ-like character	For effective service
DEVELOP-MENT	Requires our co-operation	Involves our decision to receive and use

A Christian exercising gifts of the Spirit without the fruit of the Spirit, especially love (1 Cor. 13.1-3) can be dangerous and monstrous, if not false. A Christian who bears the fruit of the Spirit but refuses to use the gifts of the Spirit has limited power and effectiveness.

Fourthly, the issue of speaking in tongues raises several problems. Do all speak in tongues? Are tongues always languages? Could tongues be of the devil? Some would counsel against it and many would avoid the issue in order to avoid divisions. These are all valid concerns.

To the series of questions in 1 Cor. 12.29-30 'Are all apostles?... Do all speak with tongues?...', the obvious answer is no. Yet, from 1 Cor. 14.5, speaking in tongues seems a real possibility for every

Christian. Furthermore, Paul could claim that he spoke in tongues more than the noisy, disorderly tongue-speaking Corinthians (1 Cor. 14.8) though, in church, he would rather speak five words with his mind, in order to instruct others, then ten thousand words in a tongue (1 Cor. 14.19). When, then, did Paul speak in tongues more than the Corinthians? Most likely when he prayed and praised the Lord, perhaps privately. In other words, tongues as a ministry gift requiring interpretation are a message *from* God, while praying and praising in tongues requiring no interpretation (1 Cor. 14.2) are directed *to* God. Tongues as a ministry gift are not given to every Christian but the gift of tongues as a prayer language is available to every child of God. Many who miss this distinction also miss the valuable gift.

The issue of tongues has been the subject of extensive investigation by both linguists and theologians. The testimonies of tongues recognised by hearers as known languages have been remarkable but not very common and are obviously outside the documented investigation of linguists. Some of the taped investigations do not meet the linguistic criteria of a language. At best, they are the 'baby talk' of the linguist or 'glossolalia' of the theologian. This need not surprise or worry us, for it is the expression of the heart of the child to the Father that matters, even though poorly verbalised for various reasons. The new expression of the Spirit delights the Father and satisfies and edifies the child (1 Cor. 14.2-4). However, there is no doubt that, very often, tongues are languages both known and unknown, for the Bible speaks of 'tongues of men and of angels' (1 Cor. 13.1).

The fear of the demonic source of tongues can be a genuine concern. Indeed, every gift of the Spirit can have a challenging counterfeit. That is why God has given his people the gifts of discerning of spirits and of wisdom. The presence and power of the Holy Spirit often unveils the presence of evil spirits in a person (Luke 4.14, 33ff, 41), in order that we may, by the power of the Holy Spirit, and in the name and authority of Jesus, set the person free. This is a big area of deliverance ministry common in the Charismatic Movement. The deliverance ministry or exorcism is not without problems, but the warning of our Lord is that deliberately attributing the work of the Holy Spirit to the work of the devil can constitute the unforgivable sin of blasphemy of the Holy Spirit (Matt. 12.22-32). A child of God who longs for and asks for the gift of the Holy Spirit has the assurance of receiving only the Holy Spirit (Luke 11.11-13).

Raphael Gasson, formerly a medium who has spoken in tongues in trances, has given some valuable insights in his book *The Challenging Counterfeit*.[4] Having experienced the spiritual dimensions of both the divine and the demonic world, he said that the devil would not be so foolish as to waste his time confusing the Churches on the issue of speaking in tongues if it were not for the fact that tongues are such a powerful gift of the Spirit for the Church.

The gifts of the Holy Spirit need not and ought not to bring division into the Church. Indeed the Spirit brings unity, and we are urged to maintain, not create, the unity of the Spirit (Eph. 4.2-3). In many instances the Charismatic Movement has brought a fresh and deeper unity between Anglicans and Roman Catholics, and has broken down denominational, social, cultural and other barriers. It is the unwise use of the gifts of the Spirit or the insistence on a particular form of charismatism, often by immature Christians, that brings divisions. Every gift can be abused and the solution of abuse is not disuse but proper use. The book *Come, Holy Spirit* by Bishop David Pytches[5] is particularly useful and is strongly recommended for those who would exercise the gifts of the Spirit. Needless to say, the rejection of the gifts of the Spirit, especially by leaders of the Church, is a sure cause of division.

A WAY OR THE WAY?

Is this *a* way or *the* way? This is a question that has been asked by countless people in all sorts of situations down the ages. Where are we going? How are we going? How quickly can we get there? What price are we prepared to pay? Who else is going with us? Do all roads indeed lead to Rome? Perhaps the question is in danger of dying the death of a thousand definitions.

Our Lord Jesus Christ made an exclusive claim: 'I am the way, the truth, and the life; no one comes to the Father, but by me' (John 14.6). The apostles Peter and Paul echoed the same truth: 'And there is salvation in no one else, for there is no other name under heaven given among men by which we must be saved' (Acts 4.12). 'For there is one God, and there is one mediator between God and men, the man Christ Jesus' (1 Tim. 2.5). Yet there are counterclaims by various religions which put forth alternative ways, basically men's attempts at getting right with God, or getting back to God. If we cannot or will not subscribe to the exclusive claims of Christ concerning God's prescribed way, then the following pages are of little relevance or consequence.

It is interesting to note that early Christianity was not regarded as a religion but as 'the way' (Acts 9.2, 19.23, 24.14). If we decide to be true disciples of Christ, to learn and to follow him as the early disciples did, then the way of the Holy Spirit is not optional. The gifts and power of the Holy Spirit experienced in the so-called Charismatic Movement become part of the Way, even though some of us had resisted or persecuted the Way as Paul had done (Acts 22.4).

If renewal is understood to include changes or renewal in various dimensions including the renewal of forms and structures, then the Charismatic Movement must remain as but a Way. But if renewal is confined to renewal in the spiritual dimension, then the Pentecost experience or baptism in the Holy Spirit, so central to the Charismatic Movement, becomes with the Charismatic Movement the way of renewal, at least for the Anglican Church. Recently, there has been an increasing number of Christian leaders who have had the Pentecost experience and who are exercising the gifts of the Holy Spirit in their ministry, e.g. in healing, and yet do not wish to come under the Charismatic label. So they form what is called the *Third Wave*. If the Charismatic Movement does not include the Third Wave, then it becomes a way of renewal. In any case, the baptism of the Holy Spirit or Pentecost experience is the essential key in the way of renewal.

The setting and background of the opening verses of Acts 1 make the parting words of our Lord in Acts 1.8 the blueprint for the Church and for renewal with a purpose and direction. 'But you shall receive power when the Holy Spirit has come upon you, and you shall be my witnesses in Jerusalem and in all Judaea and Samaria and to the end of the earth.' The purpose is world evangelisation – the fulfilment of the Great Commission which has not been withdrawn from us. The key to this fulfilment, a superhuman task, is the power of the Holy Spirit demonstrated at Pentecost and thereafter. The direction is missions (in the biblical sense) in an ever-widening circle of witnessing or sharing of our first-hand experience of the Lord from our home or home town, to our neighbourhood and to the ends of the earth. The pattern is simply that of our Lord – preaching, healing and deliverance (sometimes called exorcism). This is the desire of our Lord, for he has set us a pattern and said, 'As the Father has sent me, even so I send you' (John 20.21), and again, in John 14.12, 'he who believes in me will also do the works that I do; and greater works than these will he do, because I go to my Father.' The Book of Acts beautifully unfolds for us the result of pentecostal experience in terms of power evangelism through preaching, healing and deliverance – the same pattern of ministry as that of our Lord Jesus unfolded for us in the Gospels. This is not just a view often labelled evangelicalism. It is the main purpose of renewal and the main purpose for the Church. We cannot improve upon the ministry of the Lord; neither does the Holy Spirit. He simply enables us to continue the pattern of the ministry of our Lord. This is not just the preferred way of the Charismatics: it is the prescribed way of the Holy Spirit. We believe it is the way for our Church.

We believe that everyone who has experienced the power of the Holy Spirit in pentecostal fashion will not prefer any other way of renewal. However, this is not the same as forcing our views on our brothers and sisters in Christ. Everyone is entitled to his opinion and is answerable to the Lord one day. But to regard the baptism of the Holy Spirit simply as *a* way of renewal may well be a way of escaping from intellectual or theological problems, a way of maintaining the *status quo* so that we can continue to do our own ecclesiastical business, or what is worse, a way of disobeying the Lord or rejecting his gifts.

We come from different backgrounds and traditions, sometimes labelled Catholic, Evangelical, Liberal, Charismatic and so on. Each has a valuable contribution to make to the life and function of the Church, e.g. the authority of the Church and liturgy, the authority of the Word and evangelism, social concern, and emphasis on the Holy Spirit. Perhaps the question is not that of *a* way or *the* way of renewal. The issue is not that we should be unclothed but that we should be further clothed. Which child of God will not want the genuine gifts of the Holy Spirit? Which servant of the Lord will not want more gifts from him so that we can be more effective for him? The superhuman task of world evangelisation requires the promised supernatural power of the Holy Spirit. Refusal of this power is not mere folly, like pushing the car instead of driving it. In the ultimate analysis it is downright rebellion, because rejection of his gifts of power is, in effect, telling God to keep his gifts so that we can do it in our own way. Remember the words of Isa. 55.8-9. We may not fully understand everything but we believe we have known and seen enough to ask and receive. The proof of the pudding is in the eating. Ours is not to figure out the recipe, ours is to enjoy the pudding.

NOTES

[1] Walter J. Hollenweger, *The Pentecostals.* Minneapolis: Augsburg Publishing House, 1972.

[2] Kilian McDonnell, ed., *Presence, Power, Praise.* Vols. I-III. Minnesota: Liturgical Press.

[3] D. Martyn Lloyd-Jones, *Joy Unspeakable.* Eastbourne: Kingsway Publications, 1984.

[4] Raphael Gasson, *The Challenging Counterfeit.* Logos, New Jersey, 1966.

[5] David Pytches, *Come, Holy Spirit.* London: Hodder & Stoughton, 1985.

5

Guidance of Charismatic Experience:
New Testament Evidence and Implications for
Today

Frederick H. Borsch

There is no doubt that in Jesus' time and in the life of the early
Church a number of events regarded as extraordinary took place.
There is also no doubt that many early Christians interpreted these
events as indicative of the will and purpose of God. Twentieth-
century charismatic renewal movements are right to point to these
activities as having an important place in the beginnings of Christian
faith and practices. In particular, the healing acts and exorcisms of
Jesus may be said to be crucial. While earlier in this century a
number of critics suggested that many of these miracles were later
additions to the stories told about Jesus, it is now generally agreed
that in association with Jesus' ministry, 'There must have been cures
of various types of sickness which were amazing at least to people at
that time.'[1]

What is not as clear is the role the miraculous was meant to have
in Jesus' ministry. Not only are there different strains of tradition in
this regard, but a careful reading of the Gospels discloses what seems
to have been a complex attitude on Jesus' part. Nor is it obvious
from the study of the late New Testament period and beyond that
miracles were meant to play an ongoing role in Christian life and
witness, and, even if so, how they were to be interpreted. In this
generation, which has experienced the results of revolutions in
historical and scientific understanding, we must also recognise that
we view and understand supernatural events as described in the Bible
rather differently from first-century people. We are also aware of
how easy it is to look back and, when reading such stories from
within the horizons of our own time and world perspectives, to

misconstrue their significance for the individuals who first experienced these events and their telling and retelling.

It is not the purpose of this essay to try to reflect on all the New Testament evidence for miraculous and charismatic activities. That has been done well in recent years and some consensus points have emerged.[2] Our purpose will be to highlight what seem to be the more important questions for contemporary disciples who are guided by the Bible and to suggest responses to these issues.

MIRACLES IN THE NEW TESTAMENT

As they do with other of the strands of early traditions the several evangelists give their own emphasis to the miracle stories of Jesus. This was not only inevitable but as it should be. In different cultural, pastoral, liturgical and missionary contexts Christians have used and always will use the Gospel materials somewhat differently. The diversity of presentation in the New Testament is itself an important guide (which may well be regarded as a gift of the Holy Spirit) for contemporary preaching and teaching.[3]

We may observe Matthew cutting back on narrative detail and offering more dialogue, stressing themes of faith and discipleship along with the picture of Jesus as Lord of the world of nature and history. Luke also is inclined to play down any suggestion that Jesus could not do miracles at will. He adapts the stories to a more Hellenistic audience and presents them in a more historical perspective in which they are seen as evidence that the Spirit of God was with Jesus — a theme which is, of course, developed with respect to the missionaries of the early Church in the Acts. For the fourth evangelist the miracles are *signs* which manifest Jesus' glory and enable both early and later disciples to believe in him (John 2.11; 20.30-31).

The Johannine understanding of the miracles stands in at least some tension with the teaching of the synoptic Gospels which insist that no *sign* will be given to this generation. This saying, found in both Mark (8.12) and in the tradition common to Matthew and Luke (Matt. 12.39, 16.4; Luke 11.29, with the added words 'except the sign of Jonah' has often been regarded as a clue to Jesus' attitude. Miracles were not events designed to create belief among the otherwise incredulous — to prove to them that God's kingdom was breaking into the world. Rather were they symbolic events for which the synoptics prefer a word we may translate as 'acts of power' (*dunameis,* from which our word dynamite) to signs (*semeia*). They are revelatory of the character of God's activity in making whole and overthrowing the power of evil. Although they certainly can strengthen faith and hope, they are meant more to speak to people who have faith and hope in order that they may see what the kingdom is like. Those who 'repent' (that is have a new way of seeing and hoping, *metanoia*) recognise that these are the signs which inaugurate the new age. In another saying, which may well come from the core of the tradition,[4] Jesus tells the disciples sent by the questioning John the Baptist, 'Go and tell John what you hear and see: the blind receive their sight and the lame walk, lepers are cleansed and the deaf hear, and the dead are raised up, and the poor have good news preached to them' (Matt. 11.4-5; Luke 7.22).

Any Jewish person of the time would have recognised these words as a compendium of prophetic hopes for the messianic age (cf. Isa. 29.18-19, 35.5-6, 61.1). The acts of power signal that this age is begun in association with Jesus' ministry. Each act is important not so much in and of itself, but for what it tells about the new time begun now. They are used for teaching and often in controversy to help characterise what is happening. Many of them seem directed against oppressive religious, social and ideological practices.[5]

The story of Jesus' temptations helps interpret the significance of the miracles as well as the nature of his ministry. He could try to be a popular and sensational Messiah by performing wonders of feeding people, demonstrations of worldly majesty, and acts of supernatural power. In its own way John's Gospel carries forward the recognition that the crowds misunderstood signs, concentrating, for instance, on the bread alone rather than what it also signifies. It may, however, be Luke's Gospel which offers the most profound insight in this regard. By placing the temptation to leap from the temple pinnacle third and last, Luke indicates that the use of supernatural power to do miracles is the most subtle and greatest temptation for Jesus. With such power one could compel minds and spirits. Jesus refuses.

These are not just fine distinctions. According to Matthew's Gospel, it is not only an evil but an *adulterous* generation that seeks a sign. Adulterous is here used in the Hebrew scriptural sense to mean having relationships with false gods. It is perhaps all too human to be a sign-seeker, but to make this prominent in one's religion is to be looking for another god than the God of the Bible. The greatest danger to true faith and religion has always been superstition, especially dangerous because it may look like piety. Such superstition seeks to put divine power into human control so that by the power of human *religion* signs and miracles can be performed according to human will, to prove religious claims. It is not that acts of power do not happen, but always they must be interpreted by faith in the context of hope in the purposes of God's kingdom.

Mark's Gospel is a sustained critique of disciples who misunderstand the power of the kingdom and do not recognise the necessity of suffering and service before there can be glory. Peter is called 'Satan' for questioning the *mustness* of the rejection and death of the Son of Man (8.31-33), and James and John, and then all the disciples, are told of the primacy of suffering and servanthood (10.35-45). More surprising still is the lack of resurrection appearances at the end of the Gospel. Mark concludes the story of Jesus with the disciples pointed to Galilee, the land of mission and service, where Jesus will one day be seen coming in glory for judgement. In the meantime, however, disciples must live in hope rather than glory, following in the way of the cross (8.34).

A half-generation before Mark's Gospel was written Paul had dealt with similar issues in Corinth. Evidently some of the new Corinthian converts had understood their new life in Christ and the gift of the Holy Spirit in terms of phrases like 'Already we are filled! Already we have become rich! We reign as kings'. (See 1 Cor. 4.8). They apparently made fun of Paul for his relative lack of charismatic power and gave great heed to leaders whom they believed showed more spiritual authority. Paul archly refers to them as 'these superlative apostles' (2 Cor. 11.5, 12.11). These 'healthy' sun-tanned, apostles'[6] direct from the holy city of Jerusalem may well have been working miracles in Corinth while Paul was stuck away in Ephesus unable to cure his own lousy disability, his 'thorn in the flesh.' Three times he prayed to the Lord that it should leave him, but he was told, 'My grace is sufficient for you, for my power is made perfect in weakness' (2 Cor. 12.7-9).[7] Paul had to learn and then share with the Corinthians the awareness that every story of faithful discipleship must reflect something of the story of Jesus' suffering and powerlessness. It is not that disciples seek suffering for its own sake. What they seek are opportunities for caring and service, with which inevitably come challenges and tribulation. But amid such circumstances the true power of God is made known, 'made perfect in weakness'.

Once this understanding is placed at the heart of the presentation of the Gospel, Paul can then also remind the Corinthians that when he was with them 'the signs of a true apostle were performed among you in all patience, with signs and wonders and mighty works' (2 Cor. 12.12). But seeking after signs and wanting to make religious faith in some sense dependent upon miracles is the way of worldly religion – the way not of God but of men. Yet, while not at the service of human religion, God's power is active in the world, healing and making known the divine purpose of overcoming evil and oppression.

While a power of God which most manifests itself in the context of shared suffering and service, but yet also breaks forth in might to heal and cast out evil, must seem at the least mysterious if not paradoxical, we can perhaps gain some better understanding of its manifestations by asking about the character of this power in the Gospels. Important to notice in this regard is what is not described. Unlike a number of other stories of the time the gospel narratives rarely pay much attention to the means by which the healing is accomplished.[8] We do not hear about amulets, magical formulas, or potions. Jesus does not have to go back to the boat or into the house to get the means to heal. Hearers of the stories thus realise that the power is personal with him.

Many of the stories tell of his forgiving sins and reaching out in acceptance to those who were on the fringes of the society or even treated as outcasts because of their professions, way of life, or physical conditions. Not everyone in those times would have regarded disease or disability as the result of sin and a sign of divine disfavour, but that attitude was far from unknown.[9] One of the strongest reminiscences of the disciples about Jesus is that he was often out among those regarded as unacceptable, offering them inclusion in the kingdom, forgiveness and healing. Nor does his message seem to have been that they needed first to reform and then be accepted.[10] This more traditional religious message would probably have caused little controversy with Jesus' contemporaries. But, acting in the name of God's purposes in the coming kingdom, Jesus both by word and action offered inclusion, forgiveness and healing. A paradigm story in this regard is that of the spiritual and emotional healing of Zacchaeus who, once he finds he can be included, then in new hope is repentant and sees a new life for himself (Luke 19.1-10).

We do not have enough information or insight to be able to say that all of Jesus' healings were the result of such words and deeds of acceptance, but this seeking of the otherwise lost and outcast and including them in the offer of God's kingdom may offer the best clue into the nature of his power to heal. Some critics may worry that such an understanding is too *psychological* and prefer interpretations that seem more supernatural. They could well point, for example, to the instantaneous or near-instantaneous effects of Jesus' forgiving, exorcising and healing actions. Certainly they are right to remind readers of the New Testament that there is much that cannot be explained only on the basis of our contemporary understandings of the power of acceptance, caring and forgiveness. Yet it would also be a mistake to undervalue this clue, for it is the best and most consistent one the Gospels offer. God's concern for the making whole of God's creatures is expressed through human life. In this sense it is both natural and supernatural. In Jesus the disciples perceived a distinctive focus of that power, helping them to glimpse through his humanity the divine character of love.

MIRACLES FOR DISCIPLES NOW

How then should later followers of Jesus try faithfully to respond to the stories of healing and other miracles which are so integral a part of their foundational scriptures? This issue was already a problem for second- and third-century Christians who were not able with any frequency to replicate the kind of miracles they heard about in the Gospels and in apostolic times. They worried that this might be a sign of God's disfavour or their own unfaithfulness. Or it could mean that the Spirit of God worked differently in different eras.[11]

For late twentieth-century disciples the problems are, of course, still more acute. We recognise that the revolutions in historical and scientific understanding have greatly altered the ways in which almost all people hear the Bible and look out upon the natural world. Only two hundred or so years ago rain, earthquakes, good harvests, plagues, even eclipses were thought by many to be literal 'acts of God,' caused by direct divine intervention. There were arguments within congregations as to whether lightning rods should be put on top of churches. Opponents called them 'heretic rods', and their advocates were accused of having too little trust in God's protection. But over the years growing numbers of people found it more credible to search for ways of interpreting extraordinary happenings without recourse to belief in divine intervention in the natural processes of the world. Since it was difficult to find any instances of modern-day intervention, by historical analogy the stories of the New Testament were often explained as various forms of legend or psychological projection.[12] While some writers would still try to leave room for direct action by God by reminding us of the gaps in our full understanding of natural processes, or reflecting on the mysteries of the principle of indeterminacy and evident lack of absolute law in quantum physics, most observers, living in the macrophysical world, where a closed system of causes and effects seems to apply, do not use the explanation of divine intervention to interpret otherwise inexplicable events.

Among those who try to be faithful disciples one can see two more or less extreme reactions to these conditions. Some, of course, virtually neglect the whole biblical tradition of miracle and find it to be only a stage in a time of more primitive religious belief. Even if they would not make a sustained argument along these lines, their avoidance of the miracle tradition in preaching, teaching, counselling and theological reflection indicates that they do not find it relevant for contemporary faith and practice.

Other Christians, however, react with a commitment which insists that an authentic Christianity must manifest in its life healings and other phenomena which at least closely parallel events described in the New Testament. Although this may result in a broad disjunction between how they live in the everyday world and their 'religious' attitudes, they nevertheless try to bring what they understand to have happened in terms of first-century miracles straight into the world of television and computer technology.

There are, however, other ways of responding to the New Testament evidence. One is to ask about the more fundamental character of what the early followers of Jesus were experiencing. Let us take, for example, the particularly difficult matter of exorcisms. Few people today believe in evil spirits as objective realities which can occupy a human mind or be driven out. But many do know what it is like to feel themselves in enslavement to forces that often overmaster their rationality and better desires. Irrational fears and angers suddenly inhibit one's good intentions for one's own life and those of others. There is a sense of alienation from close relationships, and a consequent frustration and further anger directed at self and others. There is resultant guilt and often, perhaps in disguised forms, self-hatred. At times the accumulation of these forces can seem like a veritable army or 'legion' of unfriendly forces within one, as in the Gospel story of the Gerasene demoniac (Mark 5.1-20). Sometimes the demonic urge can lead one even to physical acts of self-injury.

These inner forces can be recognised as part of the self, yet also alien to what one wants for the self. Probing reflection may help one to see that the voices through which these forces can exercise control sometimes speak in distorted tones or shapes from the past – internalised authority figures which have grown deformed and may indeed seem like ogres or demons. One longs for a power which can overmaster them, but the power seems impossible to self-generate. It may only be an extraordinary gift of love – of acceptance and forgiveness – that can enable a sense of belonging again and being lovable and so love-able for others.

There is certainly plenty of evidence that healing can take place in these terms – a healing which can sometimes be physical as well as emotional and spiritual in its manifestations. It may not happen with the frequency or predictability that disciples wish. Sometimes the healings may be only partial. This may be because modern-day disciples do not have the power of love that Jesus and some early Christians were able to communicate, but these healings can be understood as contemporary manifestations of the power of that same love in the world – ways in which the power of God continues among Jesus' followers, not intervening in natural processes but working through human beings to transform lives and circumstances.

This appreciation of how the healing power of God may be realised as still active in the world cannot, of course, answer all our questions. Nor will it seem fully satisfactory, especially to those who want to stress the evidently supernatural in their understanding of Christianity. All should continue to remember, however, that the New Testament itself (particularly Mark and Paul and apparently Jesus) strongly cautions against making the miraculous central to religion. 'Man,' Dostoevsky's Grand Inquisitor cynically maintained, 'seeks not so much God as the miraculous'.[13] He may be right, but that is all the more reason why men and women of prayer have also continued to offer warnings. As one evangelical writer recently expressed it, 'The Christian who is far more enthusiastic about miracles than about prayer, far more excited about dramatic guidance than about reading the Bible, is a believer who is running a temperature; it may make him warm, but it is not an indication of spiritual health.'[14] Too much interest in the miraculous can divert disciples from concentration on the power of God's love calling Christians to offer forgiveness and the opportunity for repentance to others and to work and sacrifice for a more just and peaceable society. The example of Jesus stands paramount. God's chief ways of reconciliation are through the suffering of compassion, service and humility. Sometimes these ways will heal, and heal in extraordinary fashion by the standards of the world, but it is these ways and not the miracles themselves which are the focus of faith. It is these ways that are the vital *charisms* or fruit of the Spirit in Christian living. As Paul describes them they are 'love, joy, peace, patience, kindness, goodness, faithfulness, gentleness, self-control' (Gal. 5.22-3).

SPEAKING IN TONGUES IN THE NEW TESTAMENT

One may make some similar observations about the phenomenon of *glossolalia* or speaking in tongues in the New Testament which has also played an important part in a number of charismatic renewal movements. There is, of course, some uncertainty in assessing the New Testament evidence with regard to what the phenomenon was. It would appear that there may have been two different, if related, phenomena – one involving an ability to communicate in human languages which one formerly could not speak, and the other an ecstatic form of verbalisation which used no known human language except in bits and pieces. The first of these phenomena is described in Luke's Pentecost story (Acts 2.1-42), although some interpreters understand it to be as much or more a miracle of hearing than speaking – the bystanders from various nations being able to understand what was being said, each in their own language. A number of scholars suspect, however, that Luke has in fact modified an earlier account of ecstatic utterance (more like what took place in Corinth) to give it a more clearly evangelical purpose and perhaps also to put a question mark beside any other form of its use. The instances of tongue speaking which are also presented as a gift of the Spirit at the time of baptism in Acts 10.46 and 19.6 are not specifically described by Luke and could be meant to be similar to what is portrayed in Acts 2 or to be a reminiscence of ecstatic speech in no known language similar to what is found in Corinth.

Paul tries to give this activity, which was especially prevalent in Corinth, a beneficial but restricted place in community life. He recognises it as a gift of the Spirit (1 Cor. 12.10, 28), which he himself uses (1 Cor. 14.10), wishes for all (14.5) and does not want to be forbid (14.39), but it is certainly better – especially for the building up of the community – to prophesy (14.1-40). One notes that the gift of tongues comes last in Paul's lists (12.10, 28). If tongue speaking is done in public, it ought to be interpreted (14.13-17, 27). Indeed, if there is no one to interpret, the tongue speakers should be silent (14.28). One gains the impression that Paul really feels that tongue speaking should be reserved for private prayer. Yet, for pastoral and perhaps political reasons, he does not want entirely to undercut this public aspect of Corinthian enthusiasm.

Several interesting observations emerge. Paul does not explain or define tongue speaking, probably because it was such a well-known phenomenon – current practice in other religions. The mind of God or the gods was thought to take possession of the individual and speak in a language or in a language-like way which was not known on earth. It was sometimes thought to be the language of heavenly beings (so 1 Cor. 13.1, 'tongues of ... angels'). While not all Christians have the gift (12.30) – and one should certainly remember all the places in the New Testament it is not mentioned – it can play a useful, if restricted, role. Paul refers to it as a sign, not for believers (it is evidently not meant to make them grow in belief), but for unbelievers (14.22), though with no indication that it will convert them.[15] Clearly Paul is worried that the phenomenon wrongly used could in fact bring the church into discredit (14.23). He repeatedly stresses the need for a use of gifts that will upbuild and edify the community (14.3-5, 17, 26; cf. Rom. 14.19, 15.2; 2 Cor. 12.19).

SPEAKING IN TONGUES TODAY

Tongue speaking does not have the central place that healing had in the New Testament period and often in subsequent Christian life, but it did play an important role at significant junctures. Twentieth-century disciples can again present themselves with the stark alternative of rejecting the phenomenon altogether as a form of primitive religion or of trying to emulate it as they believe first-century Corinthians and others experienced it. Once more, however, there is at least another option. The essential character of tongue speaking seems to be a state of mind filled with a sense of God's presence. In joy or awe or both mixed the mind does not know what to say, but still feels the urge to articulate. It is an experience at least comparable to that of a person in love who finds it good to sing what are *nonsense* syllables (though they may be thought to be full of meaning) or virtually to babble. A friend hearing this may, however, have at least a fair sense of what is being felt. In a way it may communicate better than normal language.

One suspects that many Christians have had experiences along these lines when at prayer – perhaps in a time of great joy or deep anguish, or when overcome by a sense of the presence of God. Such times are at least very kindred to what Paul described as 'the Spirit helping us in our weakness; for we do not know how to pray as we ought, but this very Spirit intercedes for us with sighs too deep for words' (Rom. 8.26); or, as another translation (NEB) renders it, 'through our inarticulate groans the Spirit himself is pleading for us'.

CHARISMATIC MOVEMENTS PAST AND PRESENT

Through the Christian centuries there have been a number of charismatic renewal movements. A common denominator among them has been a sense of direct religious experience. This experience is not mediated through any hierarchy or even necessarily through particular sacraments. In their sense of direct contact with the Holy Spirit the participants have also tended to collapse history and to feel a closeness with the early disciples which at least partially overcomes problems of historical understanding. Especially in modern times this has also meant a feeling of being able to interpret the Bible without any great need for historical-critical method or help from official church teaching.

Often there have been considerable gains for discipleship and ministry through this sense of the unmediated presence of the Spirit of God. The movements have tended to be strong in times when Churches have emphasised formal structures and been inclined to restrict any full sense of ministry to the clergy. Charismatic renewal (whether emphasising the full spiritual baptism of all Christians or a special experience of baptism in the Spirit) has given to many Christians a sense of themselves as *gifted* and authorised to tell of their own Christian experience, of healing and the forgiveness of sins, to master sinful tendencies, sometimes to teach, and so forth. Frequently the experience has brought Christians together into communities with strong feelings of personal care and joy.

Every student of and most participants in charismatic renewal movements are also aware of problems: dangers of a sense of spiritual superiority, excessive emphasis on individual salvation and salvation out of rather than in the world – with consequent lack of emphasis on social justice – divisiveness, and so forth. The First Letter to the Corinthians is in many ways a pastor's attempt to walk a fine line between not wanting to undercut spiritual exuberance and zeal among the Corinthians, while yet insisting that their goal in every case must be the upbuilding of the whole Christian community. Love is always to be the end, the product and test of life in the Spirit. It is, of course, to these Corinthians in this context that the famous passage on love (12.31 – 13.13) is directed.

Many Christian leaders have found themselves trying to walk that fine line since – wanting to recognise valuable gifts of the Spirit among all Christians, yet also knowing the importance of some forms of institution, authorisation for specific kinds of ministerial responsibility, the role of sacraments, and a sense of church history and tradition. They are aware that there has always been a tension between emphases on the Church as an institution (requiring structures for continuity and identity) and the Church as a Spirit-filled and led community.[16] These leaders in their turn, however, need regularly to be reminded and to remind themselves of the always prevalent tendency to attempt to reserve unnecessary degrees of authority and position for a hierarchical and professional class of clergy, cloaking all too human proclivities for security and aggrandisement in pieties and forms of paternalism to the detriment of the growth of individual Christians, genuine community and mission.[17]

Important to reflections in this regard are the models of the Church which guide polity and practice. The model of the Church which begins, as it were, from above, with hierarchy and authorisation for ministry always being passed down from God the Creator and the Lord Jesus through apostles and bishops to other clergy and finally to laity, will probably always limit the sense of empowerment and ministry for other Christians. A more helpful and more biblical model is that of the body of Christ – the Church as a community gifted by the direction and indwelling presence of the

Spirit of the Lord, which Spirit then helps create forms of continuing leadership and direction. Such a model better allows for necessary forms of church governance and historical continuity without denying the powerful nearness of God to all Christians.

NOTES

[1] Hans Küng, *On Being a Christian* (New York: Doubleday & Co., 1976), p. 229. For a useful statement with regard to the centrality of the healing ministry in the Gospels and to Jesus, see Pierson Parker, 'Early Christianity as a Religion of Healing', *The Saint Luke's Journal of Theology* 19 (1976), pp. 142-50.

[2] See the study by John Koenig, *Charismata: God's People* (Philadelphia: Westminster Press, 1978), and J. D. G. Dunn, *Jesus and the Spirit: A Study of the Religious and Charismatic Experience of Jesus and the First Christians as Reflected in the New Testament* (Philadelphia: Westminster Press, 1975).

[3] This point is well made by James Barr in *The Scope and Authority of the Bible* (Philadelphia: Westminster Press, 1980), pp. 109, 111-113.

[4] On the passage as part of the core tradition cf. R. H. Fuller, *A Critical Introduction to the New Testament* (London: Duckworth, 1966), p. 101.

[5] See F. H. Borsch, *Power in Weakness: New Hearing for Gospel Stories of Healing and Discipleship* (Philadelphia: Fortress Press, 1983), particularly chs. 2, 4, 5, 6.

[6] For this description of Paul's opponents see Krister Stendahl, *Paul Among Jews and Gentiles and Other Essays* (Philadelphia: Fortress Press, 1976), p. 46.

[7] For a fuller reflection on this incident see Borsch, *Power in Weakness,* pp. 111-127.

[8] See Borsch, *Power in Weakness,* pp. 40-42.

[9] So in the Qumran appendix to the Manual of Discipline: 'Every person smitten in his flesh, paralysed in his feet or hands, lame or blind or deaf, or dumb or smitten in the flesh with a blemish visible to the eye, or any aged person that totters' is excluded from the congregation of holiness (1 QSa 2.5-10); and see John 9.2, 34.

[10] On this point see E. P. Sanders, *Jesus and Judaism* (Philadelphia: Fortress Press, 1985), p. 271.

[11] See G. W. H. Lampe, 'Miracles and Early Christian Apologetic', and M. F. Wiles, 'Miracles in the Early Church' in *Miracles: Cambridge Studies in Their Philosophy and History,* ed. C. F. D. Moule (London: A. R. Mowbray & Co., 1965), pp. 203-18, 219-34.

[12] On the development of the critique of the New Testament miracle stories during the past three centuries, see Ernst and Marie-Luise Keller, *Miracles in Dispute: A Continuing Debate* (Philadelphia: Fortress Press, 1969).

[13] *The Brothers Karamazov* (New York: Random House, Modern Library, n.d.), p. 265.

[14] Donald Bridge, *Signs and Wonders Today* (Downers Grove, Ill.: Intervarsity Press, 1985), p. 181.

[15] Paul draws an analogy in the preceding verse (14.21) with the people of Israel who would not heed the prophet Isaiah's message and were thus invaded by the foreign-speaking Assyrians, though they were still not converted.

[16] Still helpful in this regard is B. C. Butler's *Spirit and Institution in the New Testament* (London: A. R. Mowbray & Co., 1961).

[17] It is instructive to see how a leader in another renewal movement (liberation theology and practice) only really found himself in trouble with his Church's officials when his theology led him to question certain hierarchical structures. See Leonardo Boff, *Church: Charism and Power - Liberation Theology and the Institutional Church,* trans. by J. W. Diercksmeier (New York: Crossroad, 1985).

6

Renewal as seen from within a Traditional Catholic Spirituality

H. M. D. Westin

Anglicans have always claimed to be a part of the Church Catholic, and not merely a national Church or sect. As a former Archbishop of Canterbury, Geoffrey Fisher, clearly stated, there is no Anglican Faith; we have no faith but the faith of the Catholic Church. Our contemporary approach to issues, challenges and opportunities facing us must be worked at from this firm foundation. Current trends in the fields of political theories or of the social sciences must not be permitted to undermine or overthrow sound biblical teaching or long-established Anglican theological insights and practices. Truth from all sources must be welcomed, but not all ideas claiming to be true are true. Truth must accord with the life and teaching of the One who is the Truth, the Way and the Life, Jesus Christ. As St John taught, not all spirits are of God (1 John 4.1). We live in a world in crisis. In such a world false teachers abound; false prophets multiply, making a profitable living off confused and frightened people.

It has been said that part of the modern dilemma is the disappearance of the community in the Church and the emergence of radical individualism or of radical tyranny. This is a disease of Church and State. The root of this is seen as envy of God, which translates into lust for power. Hence rootlessness and tyranny are rampant.

> we face the danger that the structure of the Church will take on the forms of secular society and that the Church will employ means proper to

secular society. When the Church becomes a power structure, unless that power be the power of love, it takes on a secular character. When coercion replaces inspiration and love, the Church takes on a secular character; it can even take on the unpleasant aspects of the police state. When the officers of the Church dominate the faithful rather than become examples for the flock (1 Pet. 5.3), the Church takes on a secular character. I suppose the one thing that is clear from the New Testament description of ecclesiastical leadership is that one person does not impose his will on another ... To adopt the workings of the political society converts the Church into a power structure. It introduces politics in the vulgar sense of the term, by which I mean the manipulation of people and things in such a way that one gains and keeps office. It means that office is conceived primarily as power over others and as control, not as service, and certainly not as a function of love.[1]

There is a real need for renewal within the Church today. But renewal is of God. It is God's gift to his Church. However, we do well to remember that there can be no renewal where there is no faith, no belief, no knowledge of God. For the valley of dry bones to come to life and live again, we need the mighty intervention and power of God. Also required is the faithfulness of the prophet and the priest.

From the dawn of the Church, God has provided for the faithful means of grace and sanctification, ways in which they are equipped to be missionaries and evangelists, to be leaven leavening the community and society, to be faithful and resolute in the midst of apostasy, doubt, despair and chaos. For the last twenty-five years there has arisen within the Christian Church in North America, and in the West generally, what can only be described as a lack of faith. Certain theologians and bishops, and others occupying trusted positions within the Church, who should know better, have undermined the faith of many of the People of God. They have contributed to anger, hostility, to the undermining of faith in many members, the lambs of Christ's flock. Confusion has been created in many minds, hopelessness in many hearts. In the West, affluence also has undermined faith in God; affluence assisted by certain trumpeted social and economic theories, psychological insights and atheistic philosophies. The sheer complexity and business of life, the invasion of the average home by all the modern means of communication, have had the effect of removing prayer, Bible reading, silence and meditation from many lives. The sacraments have been neglected. What then, are we to do in our search for renewal?

PURPOSE OF LIFE

First, we must recover a sense of purpose and meaning to life. The Christian doctrine of the *summum bonum* – 'The end of life is the vision of God' – this basic teaching must be recovered. Surely for the Christian the purpose of life must be to know God, to love him and to enjoy him forever. As Irenaeus put it long ago, *gloria enim Dei vivens homo; vita autem hominis visio Dei*: the glory of God is a living man; and the life of man is the vision of God. In the last sentence of the Nicene Creed the undivided Church declares its belief in 'the life of the world to come'. Belief in the life of the world to come is belief that there is life after death, with either everlasting glory in heaven or eternal punishment in hell. 'Blessed are the pure in heart, for they shall see God' (Matt. 5.8); and again: 'follow peace with all men, and holiness, without which no man shall see the Lord' (Heb. 12.14). The Apostle Paul tells us, 'now we see through a glass, darkly; but then face to face: now I know in part; but then shall I know even as also I am known' (1 Cor. 13.12). God knows us better than we know ourselves. To him all hearts are open, all desires known, and from him no secrets are hidden. As St Augustine reminded us, God created us for himself, and so our hearts are restless until they rest in him. Without God we will never find the real meaning and purpose of life.

Jesus Christ came into the world to proclaim the kingdom of God, to ransom and redeem mankind, to reconcile us to the Father and to each other, to open to us the way into the Kingdom and to invite us to enter. Entry into the Kingdom involves a new creation, a new being; it is an invitation to a new reality, to a new order of things. 'The Kingdom was not an adjustment of the old faith, or even a reform movement. It was new, entirely new, so new that the best way to describe it was to call it a new birth.'[2]

Christian spirituality has to do with the day-to-day living out of the relationship with God which we have through our Baptism into Jesus Christ. It has to do with our striving to have the 'mind of Christ' in all things (Phil. 2.5). It has to do with our becoming like Jesus Christ (Eph. 4.13). We are not to be conformed to this world, but to be transformed (Rom. 12.2). True, we live for the present in this world, and have to work out, on a daily basis, our transformation into the likeness of Jesus Christ in the midst of our present environment, but we are destined for a life beyond this world. This we must never forget. The strident materialism of the affluent consumer society in the West, or the belligerent, godless materialism of the Marxist paradise of the East, must never be permitted to make us believe that human beings are merely physical, that all they can hope for is what they can grab for themselves here and now. Christians know better than that. Jesus Christ came into the world to open to us the Kingdom of God. At his ascension he took our manhood into heaven, assuring us that where he is, there also shall be his faithful people.

Finbarr Connolly[3] tells us that in the Church today two different spiritualities are being followed. He calls them 'traditional spirituality' and 'modern spirituality'. Both of these he conceives as 'absolutely authentic Christian spiritualities', although for historical reasons they are presented differently. He sees modern spirituality as being 'a more immanent spirituality' forged by the Spirit through men and events. Its emphasis is on the Church as a community of love.

> The reality is the same – our sharing in God's life; but now, instead of using the idea of 'grace', we speak of 'life in Christ' or 'life in the Spirit'. Instead of using the idea of 'virtue', we speak rather of 'the practical demands of love'. We speak of personal involvement and dialogue. Modern spirituality builds a picture of the spiritual life in terms of persons and personal realities.[4]

Be that as it may, we know from experience that it is not enough merely to belong to the People of God, to belong to community. There is more involved in Baptism than the gift of nominal membership in a community, even though that community be the Body of Christ. Nominal church membership produces a dead and lifeless Church. It not only stands for nothing and does nothing; it actually hinders the coming of God's Kingdom. The baptised must not only belong to a community, but must belong to Jesus Christ. Members of the Body of Christ are called upon to believe in Jesus Christ as Lord and Saviour, and to know him personally. Jesus said, 'I am the vine, ye are the branches: he that abideth in me, and I in him, the same bringeth forth much fruit: for without me ye can do nothing' (John 15.5). Without direct, personal contact with Jesus Christ, without his grace and daily sustenance, the leaves on the vine –

members of the Christian Church – wither, drop off and die. It is only in and through Jesus Christ that we find meaning and purpose, that we receive life itself, eternal life.

The Catholic faith has always been, and still is, that the four last things (death, judgement, heaven or hell) are the lot of all men. We all die, but death is not the end. All human beings shall stand before the judgement seat of Christ (2 Cor. 5.10; Rom. 14.10; John 5.22). The just judge sees and knows all things. According to what we are and what we have done, what we have left undone, our condition reveals us as children of God or as one of those who wilfully, deliberately and continually reject God. Those who hate Jesus and the Father (John 15.24), those who die impenitent and remain so, go to hell.

> Heaven is the blessed condition of unending happiness in the presence of God, and his holy angels and saints. The happiness of heaven consists chiefly in the sight and possession of God – the blest will 'see the king in his beauty', and that for ever and ever. It consists also in an endless reunion with all we have loved below, who have died in grace, and in our being perfectly good and holy for evermore. All who depart this life in a right relationship to God will be in heaven at last.[5]

THE WAY FORWARD TO RENEWAL

Convinced, as many within a Catholic spirituality are, by their interpretation of the New Testament and understanding of the Church's tradition, that the Charismatic Movement is not the way forward to true renewal, we must ask, what then is the way forward?

Richard Hooker is seen by many as the true father of Anglicanism. Louis Bouyer has said that his major work, *The Laws of Ecclesiastical Polity,* is perhaps the only theologico-philosophical work that could sustain comparison with St Thomas's *Summa.* He says that in Hooker's work 'the permanent features of Anglican spirituality were all prefigured.'[6] Hooker placed stress on the idea of law. To the arguments concerning Scripture and tradition, Hooker brought a third term: reason. 'By reason he did not mean an abstract dialectic but a lucid analysis of reality, and reality in its entirety, natural and supernatural, and first and foremost the historical reality in which grace was revealed to us by itself penetrating concrete human reality.'[7] Bouyer points out that no Christian theologian was ever so deliberately Constantinian as Hooker, with his idea of the Christian city – the body politic – 'achieving identification with the mystical body of Christ in as much as the members of the one were also members of the other, and the visible head of the one exercised his authority only as trustee of divine authority, submitting his empire to that of Christ.'[8] With Hooker, as with St Thomas, all law found its origin in God in the identification of the infinite will with infinite reason. Hooker saw the Church as a historical body, growing organically, not merely a free association of believers, as Zwingli held, or a society which could be reshaped from scratch according to some model picked out of the New Testament by individual exegesis, as Calvin thought.

> Modern man, having cut himself off from his roots without realising that he had thereby become a prisoner of his more recent past, could not confront revelation alone, without intermediary, nor be a sovereign judge of what revelation did or did not impose. It was tradition that judged this and imposed itself on his interpretation of Scripture, so long as it did not show itself to have deviated into a formal denial of Scripture. What interests us here is the spirituality enshrined in this conception which Hooker further developed in the fifth book of Ecclesiastical Polity, in the commentary justifying the Anglican retention of Catholic institutions such as the liturgy and the sacraments. Not only did he reintegrate the sensible and the social within the spiritual life, but also the rational, grace not at all replacing nature but healing it and raising it up. This raising up (following the Greek Fathers) was seen as the image's illumination, purification and union, in which the cross is never absent, no, but everything is absorbed not in its heart-rending paradox, but in the peaceful serenity of an anticipated resurrection, as with St John.[9]

Surely we have here, in Richard Hooker, the way forward to Renewal.

Anglican spirituality, enshrined in sermons and in poetry, owes much to such people as John Donne, Jeremy Taylor, Lancelot Andrewes (called 'the spiritual masters of Anglicanism'), Izaak Walton, Sir Thomas Browne, Herbert, Vaughan, Traherne, Crashaw. Much is also owed to Nicholas Ferrar and the community at Little Gidding, where life was dedicated to union with Christ. At Little Gidding 'people lived for nothing but to be alone with God, and the love of Christ penetrated all other love to the point of submerging it.'[10] Jeremy Taylor (1613-1667), in a day when use of the Prayer Book was forbidden, excelled in reproducing its spirituality and relating it to human life. Lancelot Andrewes (1555-1626) was one of the chief translators of the King James Bible. In the Bible and the Book of Common Prayer we find manifested the classical

Anglican expression of worship, so productive of Anglican spirituality. Here we find a disciplined approach, here we find prayer and sacramental practice providing both for common (corporate) prayer and individual prayer. The temptation – and it is very much with us today – is to dissolve this balance; to emphasise and exalt the community at the expense of the individual or to do the opposite, and stress excessive individualism to the detriment of the community.[11]

The object or goal of the spiritual life is the beatific vision, to see God as he is and to enjoy him for ever. This is when the faculties of the soul, hallowed by the discipline of devotion, will enjoy God thoroughly and completely. The Liturgy of the Church is a magnificent instrument to provide the framework where Christ himself is continually kept before us and confronts us. We must be reminded that we are called, individually and collectively, to live the life in Christ. The sacraments and sacrifice of Christ hold us and guide us. But entry into the Kingdom is a free gift of God. 'Fear not, little flock, it is your Father's good pleasure to give you the Kingdom' (Luke 12.32). The rational perception of God, when we shall know even as also we are known (1 Cor. 13.12), when we shall receive the crown of righteousness, laid up for all that love the Lord's appearing (2 Tim. 4.8), that glorifying righteousness, which will abide perfectly in us for ever, cannot be ours in this life. We are totally dependent upon the salvific work of God in Jesus Christ. Richard Hooker speaks of three kinds of righteousness, in his Discourse *Of Justification:* 'There is a glorifying righteousness of men in the world to come; and there is a justifying and a sanctifying righteousness here. The righteousness, wherewith we shall be clothed in the world to come, is both perfect and inherent. That whereby here we are justified is perfect, but not inherent. That whereby we are sanctified, inherent, but not perfect.'[12] We are justified through faith in Christ, but this is not all there is to spiritual life in this world. Cranmer himself says this in his Homily on Salvation.[13] On this point, Richard Hooker writes:

> St Paul doth plainly sever these two parts of Christian righteousness one from the other. For in the sixth to the Romans thus he writeth, 'Being freed from sin, and made servants unto God, ye have your fruit in holiness, and the end everlasting life.' 'Ye are made free from sin, and made servants unto God'; this is the righteousness of justification: 'Ye have your fruit in holiness'; this is the righteousness of sanctification.

By the one we are interested in the right of inheriting; by the other we are brought to the actual possession of eternal bliss, and so the end of both is everlasting life.[14]

Hooker goes on to argue that sanctification is the work of the Holy Spirit in us, who plants the Christian virtues in the soul, and who causes them to bring forth good works. Hooker says that his doctrine:

sheweth plainly how the faith of true believers cannot be divorced from hope and love; how faith is a part of sanctification, and yet unto justification necessary; how faith is perfected by good works, and yet no work of ours good without faith: finally, how our fathers might hold, We are justified by faith alone, and yet hold truly that without good works we are not justified.[15]

In his *Holy Living,* Jeremy Taylor divides his treatment of religion into three parts: the internal acts of religion, the external, and the mixed acts, part internal and part external. The internal acts of religion are the theological virtues: faith, hope and charity. The external are reading or hearing Holy Scripture, fasting, and keeping Christian festivals. The mixed acts of religion are prayer, almsgiving, repentance, and receiving Holy Communion.[16] A proper understanding and regular use of the sacraments, God-given means of grace, are integral to any Catholic approach to spirituality. The Caroline divines favoured 'frequent' communion. William Smythies, opposing the Puritan preoccupation with 'unworthy reception', declared that there was more danger in unworthy neglecting than in unworthy receiving. Isaac Barrow asked: 'is any man unworthy to obey God's command?' Julian of Norwich wrote: 'the dearworthy Blood of Our Lord Jesus Christ, as verily as it is most precious, so verily it is most plenteous.'[17] In most of our parishes it is now taught and recognised that the Eucharist is the central act of Christian worship. It is also good to see that the sacraments of Unction and Confession (Penance) are in most revised Prayer Books. Use of the Reserved Sacrament is now also very common and a great help in parish and hospital ministry. From a Catholic perspective it must also be said that the role of Religious Communities is important when discussing renewal. There must be concern for holiness of life and for what might be called a sacramental spirituality, a disciplined life, a deeper understanding of the Church as the Body of Christ, with all that this implies. What, then, is the way forward to renewal? The Catechism of the Book of Common Prayer

(Canada), calls upon every Christian man and woman to frame, for their personal use, a Rule of Life in accordance with the precepts of the Gospel and the faith and order of the Church. It requires the following to be considered:

The regularity of attendance at public worship, especially Holy Communion.

The practice of private prayer, Bible reading and self-discipline.

How to bring the teaching and example of Christ into everyday life.

How to witness boldly to faith in Christ.

What is required by way of personal service to Church and community.

How much money must be given to support the Church at home and overseas.

Kirk tells us, in *The Vision of God*,[18] that for Anthony, Cassian and Basil the purpose of the monastic life had been the vision of God. The greatest part of a monk's striving was a striving for that self-conquest which makes union with God possible. The monk's warfare was more a fighting to God than a fighting for God. The monk's interest was not so much in rescuing and conserving a fallen world, as it was in achieving the fulness of spiritual experience. St Benedict did much to change this concept. He kept the idea of warfare and service in his Rule: it is a service of God - the *opus Dei*, or work of worship. With his emphasis on *opus Dei*, St Benedict made prayer the central human activity. The prayer Benedict called for was wholly theocentric. This created more emphasis on service. The Rule of St Benedict achieved a synthesis of humanity, discipline and religion. Karl Rahner points out that St Luke depicts the Holy Spirit as the presence of Christ establishing his Church. The Spirit is 'the special gift' which brings about in the faithful, individually and collectively, the manifestations which are essential to a missionary activity which is still going on and growing, and indeed, which makes this activity possible.[19] Rahner holds that Christian spirituality draws its vitality from the salvific deed of God in Jesus Christ present in the Church, and that this is transmitted through preaching and the sacraments. That the sacraments have power to convert should never be doubted; the conversion of Charles Simeon as a result of an obligation to attend Holy Communion in his college chapel is proof enough of this fact!

Amongst the things which history should have taught us is that popular piety, lacking intellectual insight and sound doctrine, is very dangerous. Some of these dangers are superstition (in adoration of the sacred host), witch-hunting (the Inquisition as well as the Puritans), superficiality (copious accounts of visions, ignorance of the Bible), materialism (e.g. relics), subjectivism (devotion to the Sacred Heart), moralising (in preaching), emotionalism and eschatological fears.[20] Christians are a pilgrim people. The way forward is the way of pilgrimage. In one sense the Exodus always lies before us. We have to leave Egypt, leave slavery, and move out, through the wilderness, guided by God, towards the Promised Land. For the Christian the best always lies ahead. The work of renewal is the work of the Holy Spirit. He has to move and direct our hearts and minds; he has to stir up our wills so that we may will his will. But in another sense, as St Paul made clear, we can do all things through Christ who strengthens and equips us (Phil. 4.13). Asceticism and mysticism, action and contemplation, doing and suffering, achievement and gifts, possession and striving must all be held in tension. Joseph Sudbrack writes:

> Since the spiritual life, in spite of all human achievement, is always first a divine imperative, any prediction of the course of modern spirituality could only tentatively be deducted from the signs of the times and without speculative finality. Perhaps one could offer, however, the following formulations as typical of the direction of spirituality in our times: a more intensive commitment within the world, especially in the area of its social need; diametrical to that, a more intensive conscious-personal responsibility; stressing of the dialogal; and all of this in an open-mindedness that is today allowing Christianity to look more and more to other religions and even to atheism. But perhaps all this is but an expression of the one fact that today God reveals himself as perhaps never before as the hidden God. To live this with complete openness for the incalculable imperative of God is Christian spirituality.[21]

Be that as it may, parochial experience in North America appears to indicate a desire for stability, to terminate the chaotic conditions of the 1960s and 1970s and to move towards a more traditional approach to the practice of the Christian religion. Numbers of people attending church over the last thirty years have declined, with certain notable exceptions, but the commitment of those who do practise a faith has greatly increased: nor may this increased commitment be measured solely by financial contributions. The number of persons offering themselves for holy orders has also increased. It must be said, in spite of great self-satisfaction from our theological institutions, that the preparation of priests for parish ministry leaves much to be desired. In spite of the tremendous emphasis on lay ministry, spiritual renewal will depend heavily, from the human perspective, on the character and calibre of our parish priests. Most of those being ordained are equipped to 'counsel', but know nothing about spiritual direction. Most are equipped for a ministry of listening, but do not know how to administer to those in need, how to hear a Confession, or how to evangelise. Very few seem to know the value of Retreats. Most want to sit in an office, rather than visit house to house.

Martin Thornton[22] utters a warning which the Anglican Communion should take to heart. In these days of ecumenical thinking it is important that unity be not confused with uniformity. If Anglicanism is to play its part in the ecumenical movement it must be true to itself. 'Like the via media concept, the "bridge Church" idea must be seen in terms of synthesis and not of heterogeneity. The supplanting of Mattins by the "Jesus Prayer" and Evensong by the Rosary is unlikely to further the cause of reunion with Eastern Orthodox and Rome!' We also do well to note what Thornton has said about Catholic Spirituality: 'Catholicity involves a glorious complex of schools, emphases, and techniques, all founded upon the Creeds yet catering for different conditions and temperaments.'[23]

Since Max Warren's paper to the Toronto Anglican Congress in 1963, we are continually being told that we must listen to the world. It seems as if we have now become conformed to the world! In scripture we are told *not* to be conformed to the world, but to transform the world (Rom. 12.2)! What has happened to the God-given voice of prophecy in the Church, 'Thus saith the Lord'? Is there no gospel to proclaim? Until we recover the Gospel, believe it, live it, proclaim it, there will be no renewal. The Gospel of Jesus Christ must not be used simply to justify our views, but to put us in contact with eternal verities. There must be more teaching. Homilies must integrate scripture and tradition with the world around us. We must once again tap into the traditional sources of spiritual strength. We can and must be citizens of our day and age, but through traditional links we will not be swept away by current problems. This will prevent us being lost and confused, as so many are today.

Renewal can be found within scripture, liturgy, prayer and the fundamentals of our faith, in the creeds and other formularies of the Church Catholic. Church history shows us that there has always been adaptation to changing conditions, whilst remaining true to the unchanging verities. Hold true to the fundamentals; these are the anchors which hold fast in any storm, but make necessary changes. The Council of Jerusalem shows that the Church, guided by the Holy Spirit, can resolve major differences and move forward in missionary might. Doctrine and worship are essential, and must be seen as such. Structures are essential to life. Without structure there is chaos, disorder, confusion; but structures and tradition must not become narrow, rigid or fossilised. Worship, prayer and liturgy inform and transform. Liturgy prevents excessive individualism. Repetition teaches and stabilises. Worship can get dissipated through sheer diversity, too many alternatives. There is a sense of superficiality all around us today, not least in what passes for worship and preaching.

The Christian, most of the time, has to witness and live where he or she is. Too often we want to be someone else (someone more important or prominent), somewhere else (where there are greater crowds). Mobility and raising aspiration make us reject, all too quickly, the teaching of the Catechism that it is necessary for us 'to do my duty in the vocation to which it shall please God to call me'. We are jealous of one another; we try to destroy one another. 'It is required in stewards that a man be found faithful.' We are called to be faithful; this must not be confused with what the world calls successful. They are not the same. The Faith must be practised in its totality, even the parts of it we do not like - the parts calling for renunciation of self, the carrying of the cross of suffering. Love of God and love of neighbour are both required of the Christian. When those outside the Church see this truly manifested, then they will likely be drawn to the one we proclaim, Jesus Christ: then true renewal will take place. As Cardinal Léger, so well known in Africa for his work with lepers, has said:

When the Church takes account only of the present, she does nothing but change; if she looks only to the future, she does nothing but dream; only when she is conscious of being the living tradition of Christ is she truly renewed. When she considers the whole of time, past, present, and future, she gathers strength from the revelation she has received, she gives it to the present and so prepares for the tomorrow of God ...

Distrust or ignorance of tradition no doubt stirs up confusion and change, but it does not promote renewal. On the contrary, it endangers it.[24]

NOTES

[1] John McKenzie, SJ, in *Contemporary Spirituality,* ed. Robert W. Gleason, SJ, The Macmillan Co., pp. 150, 151.

[2] Finnbarr Connolly, CSSR, *God and Man in Modern Spirituality,* Theological Publications of India, 1977, p. 95.

[3] Ibid., p. 16.

[4] Ibid., p. 21.

[5] *The Catholic Religion,* Golden Jubilee Memorial Edition, p. 135.

[6] *A History of Christian Spirituality* Vol. III, The Seabury Press, p. 110.

[7] Ibid.

[8] Ibid., p. 111.

[9] Ibid., p. 112.

[10] Ibid., p. 125.

[11] For the implication of this, see *The Prayer Book* – a theological conference held at St Peter's Cathedral, Charlottetown, June 1985, St Peter Publications, pp. 27, 28.

[12] *The Works of that Learned and Judicious Divine, Mr Richard Hooker,* ed. John Keble, 7th edn (1888), Vol. III, Sermon 11.3, p. 485.

[13] P. E. Hughes, *Faith and Works: Cranmer and Hooker on Justification,* Wilton, Conn. 1982, p. 57.

[14] Op. cit., Sermon 11.6.

[15] Op. cit., Sermon 11.2.1.

[16] *The Prayer Book* - a Theological conference ... pp. 18, 19.

[17] Martin Thornton, *English Spirituality,* SPCK, p. 280.

[18] *The Vision of God,* pp. 270, 271.

[19] *Encyclopedia of Theology,* p. 1623.

[20] Ibid., p. 1631.

[21] Ibid., p. 1629.

[22] Op. cit., p. 14.

[23] Ibid., p. 12.

[24] 'Theology of the Renewal of the Church', in *Theology of Renewal,* Vol. 1, p. 28.

7

Renewal from an Evangelical 'Non-Charismatic' Viewpoint

Donald W. B. Robinson

There is widespread concern across the Anglican world about what some would call the renewal of the church. Much of the impetus behind the concern has come from the increasing influence of the Charismatic Movement over clergy and laity.[1] This movement has brought exhilaration into many lives and disquiet into others. Some congregations have experienced an exciting vitality in worship and ministry, though sometimes at the expense of traditional decorum and rubrical requirements. For all God's people the movement raises important questions about the shape of the Christian life and its expression at both the personal and corporate level. What is renewal? What precisely is the role of the Spirit in Christian experience? How does renewal relate to the gospel? Is renewal simply revival by another name? Is renewal confined to the Charismatic Movement? The questions could easily be multiplied.

However, not all Anglicans would answer these questions in the same way. This essay endeavours to examine the renewal question from a distinct perspective within the Anglican tradition, that of an Evangelical. (The term 'non-charismatic' is question-begging. All Christians share in the grace of God and are recipients of his gifts. But the term is used here to denote someone not identified with what has become known as the Charismatic Movement.) But what is an evangelical perspective? What spiritual benefit for the Church at large might be looked for from such a perspective?

WHAT IS EVANGELICAL?

The word 'evangelical' is too fundamental in its origin to be the sole property of any one grouping within a wider Christian community.

All Christians would claim to some degree or another to be 'gospel' people. However, the word has come to be associated with a particular set of emphases, a priority of convictions that is held by those who would describe themselves as Evangelicals. Many Evangelicals would give different answers to the question, 'What is an Evangelical?' The Evangelical Alliance, which represented a wide grouping of evangelically minded people, and indeed has been seen by some, we may note in passing, as a forerunner to the Ecumenical Movement, was formed in 1846 to

> assist and concentrate the strength of an enlightened Protestantism against the encroachment of popery and Puseyism and to promote the interests of a scriptural Christianity. Its dogmatic basis included belief in the inspiration and authority of the Bible, in the Trinity, in the depravity of man, in the mission of the incarnate Son of God, in justification by faith alone, in conversion and sanctification by the Holy Ghost, in traditional eschatology, in the divine institution of the ministry and in the obligation of baptism and the Lord's Supper.[2]

This formidable host of convictions no doubt reflected the mood of the times. A more recent, but not unrepresentative, view of Evangelicals is found in the introduction to the recently published *The Evangelical – Roman Catholic Dialogue on Mission 1977-1984; A Report*. The section is worth quoting at length.

> It is not easy to give a brief account of the distinctive beliefs of evangelical Christians, since different churches and groups emphasise different doctrines. Yet all Evangelicals share a cluster of theological convictions which were recovered and reaffirmed by the 16th century Reformers. These include (in addition to the great affirmations of the Nicene Creed) the inspiration and authority of the Bible, the sufficiency of its teaching for salvation, and its supremacy over the traditions of the Church; the justification of sinners (i.e. their acceptance by God as righteous in his sight) on the sole ground of the sinbearing – often called 'substitutionary' – death of Jesus Christ, by God's free grace alone, apprehended by faith alone, without the addition of any human works; the inward work of the Holy Spirit to bring about the new birth and to transform the regenerate into the likeness of Christ; the necessity of personal repentance and faith in Christ ('conversion'); the Church as the Body of Christ, which incorporates all true believers, and all of whose members are called to ministry, some being 'evangelists, pastors and teachers'; the 'priesthood of all believers', who (without any priestly mediation except Christ's) all enjoy equal access to God and all offer him their sacrifice of praise and worship; the urgency of the great commission

to spread the gospel throughout the word, both verbally in proclamation and visually in good works of love; and the expectation of the personal, visible and glorious return of Jesus Christ to save, to reign and to judge.[3]

The 'cluster of theological convictions' referred to above, which 'all Evangelicals share', are said to be those 'recovered and re-affirmed by the 16th century Reformers'. It is indeed generally true that the evangelical Anglican looks back to the Reformation as providing the model for a proper theological reading of the biblical revelation. In an age which took the sinfulness of human nature with the utmost seriousness two questions dominated discussion and debate: How is it possible for a sinner to be God's friend? By what authority may the answer to that question be known?[4] The answers to these key questions were found in the great slogans of the Reformers – Christ alone; grace alone; faith alone; Scripture alone.

In the matter of salvation, the accent falls on Christ, grace and faith. In the matter of authority, Scripture reigns supreme. Ecclesiastical tradition is not necessarily set aside; indeed Cranmer and his colleagues were careful to preserve legitimate traditions. But tradition, other than what was authenticated by the tradition of Scripture itself, was seen as serving and interpreting Scripture rather than as possessing a *magisterium* of its own. Even the Creeds are to be 'thoroughly received and believed' on the ground that 'they may be proved by most sure warrants of holy Scripture' (Article 8).

The principle of 'Scripture alone' is of far-reaching importance in evaluating any new or unusual presentation of Christian faith or practice. Reason and experience can never be denied their function, but for either of them to assume the magisterial role in the hierarchy of religious authorities would be to overturn the principle of 'Scripture alone'. Liturgy likewise, ancient or modern, must stand under the scrutiny of the Word of God. The closest of connections exists between praying and believing, between the *lex orandi* and the *lex credendi,* but both are dependent on revelation, and subject to the *sola scriptura.*

Not only the principle of 'Scripture alone' but the central evangelical convictions themselves have a controlling influence where new phenomena or experiences are to be assessed. This is especially true, for example, of the doctrine of salvation, the sinner's forgiveness and acceptance by a gracious God. In what has been described as 'a classical statement on the subject'[5] William Tyndale writes:

And when I say, God justifieth us, understand thereby that God for

Christ's sake, merits and deservings only, receiveth us into His mercy, favour, and grace, and forgiveth us our sins. And when I say, Christ justifieth us, understand thereby that Christ only hath redeemed us, brought, and delivered us out of the wrath of God and damnation, and hath with His works only purchased us the mercy, the favour, and grace of God, and the forgiveness of our sins. And when I say that faith justifieth, understand thereby that faith and trust in the truth of God and in the mercy promised us for Christ's sake, and for His deserving and works only, doth quiet the conscience and certify her that our sins be forgiven, and we in the favour of God.[6]

Where Evangelicals are conscious of their history and pedigree they are bound to look at contemporary events and movements in the Church to some extent in the light of their own experience. The English Reformers developed a theology of the ministry not simply to rebut a distorted sacerdotalism but to fashion a diligent, learned, serious, apostolically ordered ministry, concerned with the instruction and nurture of the faithful. The evangelical tradition has also had its strong experiential side. It looked for personal conversion and an inner personal relationship with Christ as Saviour. Evangelical families looked for 'the great change' in their growing children, and the best pattern of evangelical piety and family life sought to encourage and sustain personal allegiance to Christ, nurtured by disciplined devotion and scriptural study. The Evangelicals of the eighteenth century may not have been regarded by their contemporaries as 'the wonder of the world' as their clerical predecessors were described by Bishop Hall in the seventeenth century. They were regarded as being without weight of learning, yet they constantly won the admiration of those who disagreed with them, such as the Anglo-Catholic layman, George Russell, who wrote, 'The evangelicals were the most religious people whom I have ever known ... I recall an abiding sense of religious responsibility, of self-sacrificing energy in any works of mercy, an evangelistic zeal, an aloofness from the world and a level of saintliness of holy life such as I did not expect again to see realised on earth ... May my lot be with the evangelical saints from whose lips I first learned the doctrine of the Cross.'[7]

WHAT IS RENEWAL?

It is not easy to treat historically the 'spiritual renewal' referred to in the ACC-6 Report *Bonds of Affection* (pp. 77ff). The activities and phenomena are so recent and diffuse that there is, as the Report recognises, a 'problem of definition'. We stand too close to them, and they to us, for a proper analysis to be undertaken. In particular, one must question the wisdom of using the term renewal or spiritual renewal for an agglomeration of activities and changes so various and diffuse. Christian history has not lacked movements for reform, revivals, zealous ministries, innovations in worship, or tensions between formal and informal church practice. In particular, the history of 'enthusiasm' is well documented. What justifies the use of the term renewal, and the theological approbation of that term, for the whole range of activities and changes which excites our present interest?

In keeping with the principle of 'Scripture alone', the evangelical instinct is first to ask, What is the biblical presentation of renewal? The idea of renewal is certainly appealing, but where an idea has strong biblical roots we must be careful not to transfer the dignity and sanction of the biblical idea to something which may be less than what the Bible is talking about. 'Renewal' or 'making new' pervades the whole message of the New Testament, indeed the Bible. It is especially associated with words like *anakainosis, anakainoo,* and most frequently the adjective *kainos.* But in the New Testament, renewal describes the whole work of God through the gospel and salvation, not some sort of secondary, subsequent, or periodic renovation or revival in the Church. *'Kainos* is the epitome of the wholly different and miraculous thing which is brought by the time of salvation.'[8]

Briefly put, the Scriptures from Genesis to Revelation unfold the story of how God glorifies his name by bringing many sons and daughters to glory, renewing them in the image of his Son, Jesus Christ, by means of the transforming work of the Holy Spirit.[9] Biblical renewal is Trinitarian in its source: the Father sends the Son, who reconciles estranged humanity to God, and the Holy Spirit proceeds to sanctify and transform the redeemed. Biblical renewal is cosmic in scope: the created order itself is encompassed in God's saving work, as the latter section of Romans 8 declares (cf. Matt. 19.28). Renewal in this sense reaches its climax in the creation of a new heaven and a new earth (2 Pet. 3.8-13; Rev. 21, 22). But the elements of the new creation have already invaded the here and now. The Christian is a new creation (2 Cor. 5.17) and possesses the Spirit (2 Cor. 1.22-24). Yet the Spirit thus experienced is but a downpayment on what is yet to come (2 Cor. 1.22-24), the 'first fruits' of a new creation in the midst of a disordered world (Rom. 8.18-25). Thus, the Christian individual and the Christian community lives in the 'in-between' times, between the now and the not yet. The outer man wastes away, but the inner man is 'renewed' day by day (2 Cor. 4.16-18).

Even such a brief summary indicates something of the interweaving of the doctrines of Christ, of salvation, and of the last things, in a full biblical understanding of renewal. Renewal is the great Christian hope focused on the Lord who is the First and the Last.

HOW TO ASSESS?

It may or may not be true that there is a greater or more widespread grasp of this biblical understanding of salvation at the present time than in previous ages. Such an understanding is certainly not the exclusive possession of one particular group or tradition in the Christian family, nor is it linked with a particular form of churchmanship or liturgical practice or ministerial style. If there is a special evangelical contribution to the discussion of how we assess the matter, it is the insistence that the biblical view of renewal be allowed to control our thinking and our estimates, and that we do not first accept a certain state of affairs on the basis of our observation or experience and then justify it by attaching a biblical label to it.

The ACC-6 Report, in discussing the problem of definition, recognises that 'once spiritual renewal is defined in any breadth, it becomes renewal of every kind, and since renewal is of the essence of Christianity the subject really becomes authentic Christianity in all its manifestations'. But if 'authentic Christianity' is really the subject, it is difficult to see that we are in any different situation from Christians in the first or any other century. We must not believe every spirit, but test the spirits to see whether they are of God. We must receive one another, but not for doubtful disputation. We must look not to our own interests but to the interests of others. We must do all for the sake of the gospel.

Naturally in the twentieth century any changes or new ideas are likely to have far greater currency because of greatly enhanced means of communication, and we should hesitate to identify social changes (which affect the Churches no less than other parts of society) as special dispensations of the Holy Spirit. Part of our difficulty in assessing and responding to changes and new initiatives is that our traditional tests for 'authentic Christianity', I mean our articles and canons and liturgies, are not very efficient to cope with situations not originally envisaged by them, and are themselves objects of criticism and change. But we should not jump to the conclusion that being liberated from these older tests is necessarily a sign of renewal in any significant biblical sense. This is not to say that nothing good is happening. But feeling good about change is not enough, especially when one man's (or woman's) good is often another's grief.

It may be relevant here to draw attention to an alternative way of coming to terms with current changes which is suggested in the Report of the Inter-Anglican Theological and Doctrinal Commission, *For the Sake of the Kingdom,* under the heading 'Repentance and the Variety of Religious Cultures'. One need not doubt that there may be room in Christian experience for all the activities which either in a narrower 'charismatic' or a broader sense are designated as 'renewal', as there is clearly room for a wide variety of cultural expressions of Christianity. Adherence to one's own tradition should not be so rigid as to exclude the apostolic injunction to 'receive one another, as Christ received you, to the glory of God' (Rom. 15.7). The Report explores the relation of cultural diversity to the divine ordering of creation itself, and suggests that there may be need for something analogous to what the New Testament understands as 'repentance' if we are to perceive some aspect of the truth as perceived from another's background.

It still remains difficult to know what can usefully be subsumed under the heading of renewal. The Evangelical revival would be regarded by some as a 'renewal' movement. So from a different point of view was the Tractarian movement. So again was the modernist movement. Solemn conclusions were reached that adherents of all these movements could be regarded as belonging within the boundaries of the Church of England. New positions and activities may dissolve the traditional Anglican order altogether, especially if we include 'liberation' movements under the heading of renewal. But it does not follow that such changes, however sincerely or enthusiastically embraced, equal 'renewal' of a divinely approved kind. We will still be left with the counsel of St Paul: 'prove all things; hold fast that which is good' (1 Thess. 5.21).

AN EVANGELICAL PERSPECTIVE

What observations or reservations might an Anglican Evangelical have concerning distinguishable aspects of 'renewal' in its narrower sense, the Charismatic Movement? Definition remains a problem. Many within the Charismatic Movement would affirm all that has been attributed to Evangelicals, who, one hastens to add, have no monopoly of revealed truth or of its authorised articulation. On the other side, there is much associated with the Charismatic Movement which an Evangelical (not definably within it) welcomes without reserve. Some touched by the Movement would appear, to this observer at least, to have had an old-fashioned evangelical conversion! Without question, an extensive new common conversation has become possible – and fruitful – among many who formerly were at odds because of differences of churchmanship. Some of the exuberance found in Charismatic circles has, or has had, its counterpart in a similar kind of exuberance in evangelical circles particularly of the pietistic variety. It is true that where a very exuberant Charismatic ethos has 'taken over' the liturgical worship of an Anglican parish there have been real problems analogous to what has happened in the past when a parish became Anglo-Catholic or otherwise changed its churchmanship, and the solution has been only the expedient of creating yet another stream of churchmanship, with simple parishioners who merely want to 'to go to church' being constrained to join themselves to another congregation. On the other hand, where the existing liturgical tradition has been respected there has been a warmth of prayer and praise of benefit to all.

There are, however, matters of wider concern. A defining characteristic of the Movement is an accent on the exercise of spiritual gifts based on a model thought to be recoverable from Paul's Corinthians correspondence, especially 1 Corinthians 12 – 14. Such an exercise – it is argued – is usually attributed to a deep experience of the Spirit often termed 'the baptism of the Spirit'. Other terms employed to capture this experience of the Spirit include 'the release of the Spirit, the actualising of water baptism, or being filled with the Spirit'.[10] It is this experience that lies at the base of the whole

Movement. Thus, Michael Harper writes, '... the effects of that real presence ... are to be seen and felt in free worship, in signs and wonders, in changed lives and changed circumstances'.[11] This 'renewal' touches the life of the Christian both individual and corporate. Because of the vivid nature of the Spirit's presence in charismatic activity, Harper can argue that the Movement 'in some sense possesses no great incentive to provide a theological justification for its position'.[12] Indeed amongst spokesmen sympathetic to the Movement there is some disagreement about the best way to describe the experience theologically.[13] However, there would be general agreement that such an experience of the Spirit (however described) is a non-negotiable feature of authentic Christian 'renewal'.

The critical challenge of the Charismatic Movement is its claim to have discovered, for our own time, a normative Christian experience which, when embraced, changes the whole face of Christianity, personal and corporate. The claim is that the experience is the same as may be read about in certain parts of the New Testament, and is self-authenticating. Unlike the Irvingites and the first Pentecostalists who identified their *glossolalia* and other ecstatic experiences as a sign of the imminence of the End, modern Charismatics seem rather retrospective in their orientation, seeking to reproduce the conditions of the church in Corinth. Charismatic phenomena may indeed be taken as signs of the End, as in the New Testament, but signs of the End having come, rather than as yet to come.[14] Healing, for example, is held out as a present possibility for all, rather than as a sign of the Kingdom for whose coming we still pray. In broad terms, the eschatology of the Movement is strongly realised. It remains unexplained why these particular 'charismatic' phenomena should have been so rare and spasmodic in Christian history.

While the interpretation of the New Testament for the twentieth century may be nobody's strong point, many evangelical Anglicans would be doubtful that the expressions of the Charismatic Movement and the assessment given to them are based on a right understanding of the New Testament as a whole. Primitivism, or the attempt to reconstruct our church life on the model of the earliest churches (which one?), is fraught with problems, not only in respect of church polity, but also in respect of religious experience. It is by no means clear that what may be experienced today, for example 'speaking in tongues', is to be equated with experiences described by that phrase in the New Testament. Further, Evangelicals have been prone to use the cardinal Christian doctrines as the test of authentic Christianity, and some of their uncertainty about the Charismatic Movement is uncertainty about whether 'Christ alone', 'grace alone' and 'faith alone' are truly the tests of truth and experience. The doctrine of justification takes its coherence from being situated in a framework of sin and grace, with the focus on Christ as the all-sufficient Saviour and Lord. But are sin and grace the matrix for a charismatic understanding of God's saving work in Christ?[15]

RENEWAL OR REFORMATION?

Earlier in this essay the use of the term 'renewal' to describe either the Charismatic Movement or a wider stirring for change within the churches was questioned on the ground that the New Testament has a different concept in view when it uses this kind of language. Nevertheless, what is broadly intended by the modern use of the term (which has not yet found its way into Cross's *Dictionary of the Christian Church*!) must be the concern of us all. If we ask the question, by what means does God preserve and bless his people in the process of time?, we are directed to the apostolic tradition (*paradosis*) contained in the New Testament. This tradition, the means by which the life of the early churches was regulated, did not contain everything the apostles happened to say to their churches, or even all the advice they may have given them. It was in a particular way 'the word of Christ', 'the command of the Lord', 'the mind of Christ', 'the sound words of our Lord Jesus Christ' (Col. 3.16; 1 Cor. 14.37; Phil. 2.5-11; 1 Tim. 1.13). Jesus' promise of the Spirit was that he would enable the apostles to recall and comprehend what Jesus himself had taught (John 14.26, 16.12-15). The Spirit continues to enlighten us as to this word and apply it, but the touchstone is always 'the deposit', 'your most holy faith' as to belief and conduct.[16] Those who have oversight in the Church must use the 'tradition' to govern the Church. The term generally used to indicate the need for the constant fidelity of the Church – its leaders and its members – to the apostolic tradition, both in faith and order, is 'reformation'. Reformation relates to the life of the Church as a whole, and indicates a willingness to be constantly reformed by the Word of God.

One may easily gain the impression that the Charismatic Movement bears little relation *characteristically* to the criteria of the faith.

Certainly it has a warm regard for certain parts of the New Testament, but it does not appear to have a clear hermeneutical principle in the use of Scripture, and in particular no discernment of what constituted the apostolic tradition given to regulate the faith and life of the Church.

RENEWAL OR REVIVAL?

Yet orthodoxy, even reformed orthodoxy, is no guarantee of spiritual vitality. If reformation presupposes a de-formed church needing to be re-formed in faith and order, revival — to use the term traditionally employed by Evangelicals — presupposes a sterile orthodoxy needing vitality. Much of what Charismatics call renewal is what Evangelicals have tended to call revival. In evangelical history revival has been closely associated with a certain understanding of sanctification, which is the individual Christian's progress in godliness, a lifelong process of growth and transformation into the likeness of Christ by the power of the Holy Spirit. Again, there is, no doubt, a considerable area of overlap with much that Charismatics associate with renewal, for example in relation to the fruit of the Spirit as expounded in Gal. 5.16-26.

It would be profitable to examine further the bearing revival may have on the present concept of renewal. There has been considerable study and analysis of revival in evangelical theology.[17] Revival, although a matter for petitionary prayer, is not viewed as the product of human planning. The initiative lies with God. Word and Spirit both feature in revival and are inseparably connected through their common pointing to Christ as Lord of the Church. The human responses of amendment of life and faith in God's promises are themselves wrought by Word and Spirit. The Evangelical Awakening of the eighteenth century was such a revival. Another way of understanding the phenomenon of revival is to view it as 'an intensifying and speeding up of the work of grace'.[18] The marks of revival include: a profound awareness of sin, a deep repentance, an embracing of the glorified, loving, pardoning Christ, boldness of speech in his name, freedom and joy in the Lord, love for his people, and a repudiation of sin.[19] Of course God is not bound to visit his people in a way prescribed by Evangelicals! But an Evangelical who is aware of past revivals unavoidably brings that awareness to his assessment of the present renewal movement.

Perhaps the lines drawn in this essay between Evangelical and Charismatic are too precise. Much of what happens in our churches today may be traceable to this source or that but may not require to wear a badge of origin. There is evidence of love and forbearance, a receiving of one another, a willingness to listen and learn. Yet the evangelical movement in the Anglican tradition has a history of its own, and has a position which may not inappropriately be used as a measure against related but not identical movements.

NOTES

[1] As can be seen in the recent volume, David Martin and Peter Mullen (eds.), *Strange Gifts?*, Oxford 1984, especially the contributions by Gunstone and Mullen.

[2] *The Oxford Dictionary of the Christian Church*, ed. F. L. Cross, 2nd edn, London, 1974. Article: 'Evangelical Alliance'.

[3] *The Evangelical-Roman Catholic Dialogue on Mission 1977-1984: A Report*, ed. Meeking and Stott, 1986, p. 8.

[4] As John Stott cogently argues in 'The Evangelical View of Authority', *Bulletin of Wheaton College,* 45 (February 1968), p. 1; cf. P. D. L. Davis, *The Church and the Theology of the Reformers,* London 1981.

[5] P. E. Hughes, *The Theology of the English Reformers,* 2nd edn, Ann Arbor 1980, pp. 49ff.

[6] Ibid., p. 48.

[7] Cited by C. Smyth, *The Church and the Nation,* London 1962, p. 137.

[8] Behm in Kittel's *Theological Dictionary of the New Testament,* Vol. III, p. 449.

[9] 2 Cor. 2.17, 18; Col. 3.10; Eph. 4.22-24; Heb. 2.5-15, *inter alia.*

[10] Michael Harper, *Charismatic Crisis: The Charismatic Renewal, Past, Present and Future,* Mitcham 1980, p. 12. Also see a good survey of Charismatic theology by Paul S. Fiddes in David Martin and Peter Mullen, eds. op. cit., pp. 19-39.

[11] Michael Harper, *This is the Day,* London 1977, p. 57.

[12] Ibid.

[13] Harper sees the 'Baptism of the Spirit' as part of the sacrament of Baptism; whereas the late David Watson avoids the sacramental inter-pretation. For Harper, ibid., pp. 60-61, and for Watson see *One in the Spirit,* London 1973, chapter 3 especially.

[14] As Watson argues, ibid., pp. 88-89.

[15] Douglas Davies presents some interesting sociological reasons why in his opinion they are not, in David Martin and Peter Mullen, eds., op. cit., pp. 144-145.

[16] In the New Testament the word translated 'tradition' occurs only in the sense of what is transmitted, not of transmission. To go on, Paul sees no antithesis between pneumatic piety and a high estimation of tradition. The essential point for Paul is that it has been handed down (1 Cor. 15) and that it derives from the Lord (1 Cor. 11.23) (TDNT, Vol. II, p. 172).

[17] See J. I. Packer's discussion of revival in contradiction to Charismatic renewal in *Keep in Step with the Spirit,* Leicester 1984, pp. 244-248.

[18] James I. Packer, 'Puritanism as a Movement or Revival', *Evangelical Quarterly,* Vol. LII, No. 1, Jan-Mar 1980, p. 2.

[19] Ibid.

8

Renewal and the Transformation of Society

Sumio Takatsu

A brief survey of renewal in the Lambeth Reports of 1968 and 1978, and of ACC meetings to date, indicates that this is a comprehensive subject. It has to do with the Church and its members as regards their participation in the renewing work of the Triune God in the transformation of this world, under new perspectives on matters concerning faith, liturgy, church structure, mission and ministry. This is an attempt to pursue that line of understanding, bringing into this chapter the voices of those who believe that spirituality is defective without participation in the transformation of society.

THE UNIVERSAL SCOPE OF RENEWAL

Renewal is God's work. Out of the old, out of death, he brings newness of life. The story of the Bible and the Church continuously tells about God who brings life to the world by the power he displayed in the resurrection of Jesus Christ. Power and life: this is an amazing conjunction in the eyes of the common people of Latin America, from which I write. Here, power has to do with domination, and domination ends up in death. But in God power is love, and love evokes and fulfils life in relationship and universal fellowship.

If it is true that the Gospel proclaims Cross and Resurrection as the central focus of God's renewing activity, it is also true that the Church's liturgy centres on, and springs out of, God's love for the world, the sending of the Son, his incarnation, ministry, death and resurrection. In fact, the Church praises God for the ways in which he fulfils his purpose to renew the whole creation.[1] Thus the context of spirituality is the whole earth inhabited by the people of different races and cultural and historical backgrounds under the kingly rule of God, qualified as fellowship, justice and peace. This is a vision of faith nurtured by the Holy Spirit, who, in this time, gives us a fore-taste of such a banquet and an earnest yearning for its fulfilment.

THE HOLY SPIRIT WORKS FOR RENEWAL

A Brazilian theologian has stated that 'the Holy Spirit may be regarded as the One who continuously renews God's commitment towards people. By the Holy Spirit God continues to involve himself in the history of humankind, committing himself to it, intensifying his action toward the new heaven and the new earth.'[2] This statement, together with the previous reference to the Church's message and prayer, reminds us of the final Christian vision in the last book of the Bible. There, between the announcement of the new heaven and new earth (Rev. 21.1) and the promise 'Yes indeed! I am coming soon', and the earnest yearning 'Come, Lord Jesus!' (Rev. 22.20), we see a description of the marvellous city of God. Is not this new city on the new earth under the new heaven the goal of the work of the Holy Spirit? The late Professor G. W. H. Lampe said that the work of the Holy Spirit is to build up human community into the likeness of the Son. This aim is broader than the Church as an end in itself.[3]

The city is a metaphor of the possibility and yearning for fulfil-ment in human work and in our journey in fellowship; yet, at the same time, it stands for the contradiction of partnership. This is true of a city like São Paulo. A matter of ten years ago, a group of sociologists and economists made a study of the living conditions of its population. The results were published under the title 'São Paulo 1975 – Growth and Poverty'. It presented the following conclusions: 52 per cent of its population was not born in the city; they came from somewhere outside. There is an enormous accumulation of wealth in relation to the other states of the country. As wealth concentrates, poverty increases. This means that just a few people have access to the goods and possibilities the modern sophisticated industrial society can offer, while the vast majority is on the way to being reduced more and more to a sub-human condition. In spite of this contradiction São Paulo has a tremendous attraction for many millions of people in this country, so that many come to the city seeking for work, the opportunity to study, and better living conditions. Even in its frustration, a city like São Paulo seems to stand for a yearning for human fulfilment.

The Book of Revelation recognises the contradictory dimension of the existence of the city, and tells the story of the redeeming activity of the Son in the Holy Spirit surpassing and overcoming the contradiction. Therefore the city is under the promise of its fulfilment in the final consummation. For by creating and recreating the new fellowship between persons, liberating their lives and relationships from the destructive power of death, transforming the order and structures of this world, 'the Holy Spirit glorifies Jesus the Son and through him God the Father'.[4] So we can conclude that renewal is the work of the Holy Spirit for the transformation of the whole person and the whole world and for the glorification of the Son and the Father.

RENEWAL AS LIBERATION FROM IDOLATRY AND IDEOLOGICAL CAPTIVITY

Some liberation theologians speak of liberation as a struggle against idols.[5] The perversity of idolatry as they understand it is not in the attempt to make God visible. What is at stake is not visible versus invisible, material versus spiritual. God's transcendence does not exclude visible manifestations. As von Rad reminded us, Old Testament discourse on God is occasionally 'uninhibitedly anthropomorphic'.[6] Thus what is at stake is the transcendence of God understood as liberating power. In other words, idolatry is the exchange of fidelity to the liberating God for fidelity to the oppressive power. The place to read about this exchange is the story of Aaron's manufacture of a golden bull-calf and his erection of an altar to it for sacrifice in the absence of Moses, so as to take the people back to slavery (Exodus 32).

An idol is a product invested with divinity in the service of those who control production, that is, for the benefit of the oppressors and the oppressive system. That is what prophets like Isaiah and Jeremiah understood as the danger of idolatry. (Isa. 44.9-20; Jer. 10.1-16). Leonardo Boff sees the perversion of reason and power at the roots of the violence and oppression in the Third World under the rationalistic capitalist system. He writes: 'reason and power are not in the service of life'.[7] Power is corrupted by being exercised in function of the accumulation of power for its own perpetuation. Reason is corrupted in the service of rationalisation. For Boff the capitalist system of the western countries, like the technocratic economic planning of the socialist countries, moves, structurally speaking, within the same horizon of power as domination and reason as the way of giving rational legitimacy to the establishment.

Consequently, renewal spirituality demands a sensitivity to the pervasive corruption of reason, the ideological captivity that the societies in which we live suffer. One example of this is that the majority of people are inclined to think that violence always comes from below. The demand for justice which comes from the victims of social injustice is equated with violence in the minds of many people. In *The Ideological Arms of Death*,[8] F. Hinkelammert calls our attention to the fact that even those who recognise the social injustice that poor people suffer regard their demand for justice as violence when they go to the streets for protest. If there is a revolt of the less privileged ones, often violent in nature, 'it is frequently a response to the less spectacular but equally destructive violence of social injustice', the Lambeth 1968 Report reminds us.[9]

Our ideological captivity often misdirects our perception of the things which happen around us. Maria Vitoria Benevides, a Brazilian sociologist, in her survey of urban violence, makes a series of observations on cases where the poor and criminals are linked by suspicion in the eyes of privileged people and the police. She calls attention to the fact that the first thing that criminals from the slums do is to buy a new and better suit in order to mislead their victims. Also, she notes that the poor suffer discrimination even in a court, because there is a kind of 'VIP trial' reserved for the upper classes.[10] In fact, it is fair to say that social discrimination is not restricted to the economically disadvantaged. The unemployed, young dissidents, racial minorities and women suffer discrimination. So the poor and oppressed people in this part of the world live in a kind of situation in which human dignity is permanently violated, as Gustavo Gutierrez says.[11] It is a sort of institutionalised injustice with institutionalised violence. Most Christians are inclined to see this reality only from the viewpoint of the dominant class.

RENEWAL AND BAPTISMAL SPIRITUALITY

A renewal congenial to the work of the Holy Spirit has to grapple with the problem of the liberation of Christians from ideological captivity or idolatry, so that human reality can be seen through the eyes of Jesus Christ. We understand this liberation to begin at Baptism, which is deliverance into the fellowship of the people of God, for the sake of his mission by the power of the Holy Spirit through identification with the death and resurrection of Jesus Christ. Baptismal spirituality is dynamic. Basic to the dynamic of this sacrament is the growth of the ones baptised in the following of Jesus Christ and the renunciation of evil. By evil, we mean the power which prevents the access of human beings to the mystery of life and relationship experienced as the co-existence of brothers and sisters in God. The evil renounced at Baptism, according to the rites of the American and Canadian Prayer Books, also adapted and adopted for use in the Igreja Episcopal do Brasil, clearly has cosmic, inter-personal and personal dimensions. Likewise, the promise to follow Jesus Christ has missionary and social aspects. This can be seen more clearly in the baptismal covenant, renewed by the whole congregation at each baptism. In the context of the baptismal creed the promises are made to continue in the apostles' teaching and fellowship, in the breaking of bread and in the prayers, to proclaim the Gospel, to seek and serve Christ in all persons, to strive for justice and peace for all, and to respect the dignity of every person. Thus Anglican spirituality is socially orientated from Baptism.[12] These considerations compel us to say that the concept of renewal as it is spelled out in the Report of ACC-6 under the title 'Spiritual Renewal' lacks something essential for being spiritual.

Baptism is the beginning of our identification with Jesus Christ, his life and mission in his Church, an identification which means following Christ in his mission today in the power of the Holy Spirit. This is spiritual life, life after God, life after the Spirit, in contrast to life according to the flesh. Now the place where Jesus placed himself and continues to do so today, where God's Word addresses men and women, where the Spirit fights against death, is the place where the poor and oppressed people are being continually pauperised and marginalised, as the liberation theologians of Latin America point out. The significance of these theologians seems to lie in the fact that they point to that place as the place of the spiritual renewal of the Church. For Gustavo Gutierrez in his book *We Drink From Our Own Wells,*[13] for instance, the spiritual life is an experience of one's whole life being met and addressed by the Lord, who goes to the poor and delivers to them the good news of love and life. To drink from our own wells is to drink from the depth of the experience of faith. The living water is the gift of the Holy Spirit himself lived by Jesus. So to drink from his well is to live in the time of the Holy Spirit.

LIFE IN THE SPIRIT AND LIBERATION

Liberation has a political dimension. Hunger in Latin America is a good example of how politics are involved. Here 65 per cent of the population consumes less than the necessary minimum of calories. This has to do with political decision. An appendix to the Brazilian edition of *Hunger,* published by the Secretariat of the Independent Commission on International Humanitarian Issues, states: 'Hunger does not happen, but it is produced. It is necessary to analyse, therefore, the production of hunger as the work and responsibility of particular persons acting in Society. The production of wealth is more a matter of political decision than technical process. To produce is to define goals and priorities'.[14] Life for a minority and starvation for the majority, is not this a spiritual problem? However, it is probable that for the majority of churchpeople the oppression, hunger and marginalisation that people suffer may not have anything to do with spirituality. Here it is worthwhile to remember that for N. Berdyaev the hunger of others was a spiritual problem, and one's own hunger a physical one.[15] Hunger is a sign of the absence of a truly human fellowship of brethren. So politics, hunger and their relationship cannot be dismissed so easily as a non-spiritual problem.

Isn't the life of Jesus, his proclamation, and the interpretation of what happened to him in his death and resurrection, the heart of the biblical teaching? This teaching in fact makes a liberating connection between poverty, politics and spirituality.

THE BIBLICAL VIEW OF SPIRITUALITY – LIFE AGAINST DEATH

The social and political transformation of society as the implication of the Gospel faces resistance among churchpeople as not being spiritual. For many people, renewal is limited to the sphere of specifically religious life. Social, political and economic questions are regarded as 'worldly affairs', supposedly outside of God's concern. This is due, in part, to the pervasive mistaken dichotomy of body and soul. This religious dissociation is curiously in solid association with 'worldly affairs' by way of approval of its *status quo*. Whereas, to the contrary, spirituality is a matter of living with God, who enjoys the company of men, women, children, young and old in their joyful relationship of freedom, justice, forgiveness, love and peace. For the sake of this company, God sent his Son and he gave himself. Spirituality cannot be dissociated from political and economic questions.

Nowadays the liberation theologians have made an attempt to recover the biblical view of spiritual life and to recast it in the situation of Latin America.[16] They see it as Spirit struggling against death. This is a biblical way of underlining the struggle of the people in this part of the world. What is at issue in this continent is the Spirit of life and love against death as an absolute destruction of the possibility of human realisation in a meaningful community of persons in fellowship. This is a biblical notion.

Where the struggle of life against death is felt acutely, as it is in Latin America, life in the Spirit becomes a foretaste of the resurrected body, and the social implications of this become relevant. The loneliness in the midst of the crowd in modern cities – you are the victim of an assault in a crowded street, you shout for help, and nobody pays you attention – the individualism which breaks the fellowship, the coercive conformity imposed by authoritarian systems, the marginalisation of unwanted people, the domination of powerless masses by a minority in power – these are examples of the manifestation and anticipation of death.

In fact, the Gospel is the proclamation that Christ overcame death by his death and resurrection, and now we have the foretaste of his victory in the Holy Spirit in his Body. This has to be translated into the situation where the battle is poignantly fought. Truly, the Gospel which evokes and shapes spiritual life shows its evocative and shaping power where the provocative Gospel and challenging situation are put side by side. For Pablo Richard, the relevance of the Gospel is being experienced in Latin America in the place where poor people are fighting for *bread, health, roof, education* and *security*. For him these basic conditions for life are more than economic, political and ethical demands. They are rather spiritual imperatives. They are so because the fight for basic conditions of life is a fight for life and justice. The transforming power of the Gospel is that it evokes a transfiguration of this fight into an earnest yearning for that

Other with whom a truly humane community may be built, a community of peace where the relationship between persons is sustained by love for others, the security and dignity of every person are secured by justice, and authoritarian arbitrariness is replaced by dialogue and participation.

SPIRITUALITY AS LIBERATION FOR OTHERS AND SEEING THE NEW FACE OF GOD

For Gustavo Gutierrez the commitment to liberation in Latin America has brought to many Christians an authentic spiritual experience in the truly biblical sense; living in the Spirit makes us know ourselves as free children of God and brothers and sisters to one another.[17] The simple action of prayer begins to have deep meaning. Gutierrez says that it is a surprise to see people, more and more engaged in an organised and efficient manner in the struggle for life and justice, give themselves more and more also to prayer in the conviction that love and peace are gifts from God.[18] What is happening is the release of the potentiality and meaning of sacramental life in the battle for liberation.

For Leonardo Boff this new spirituality comes out of the encounter between a suffering people and the new and challenging face God reveals in the great question posed by historical reality in Latin America. His face is new in that its apprehension does not fit in a defined category within the limits of mere religion, but is revealed as a happening full of hope for the future of humanity.[19] This new vision of God expresses itself in the emergence of a new community of justice and compassion, an alternative to the politics of oppression and exploitation.[20] It is worth observing in passing that the recovery of the biblical message by those who teach the Bible in universities and seminaries meets the concern of those who are interested in spirituality as transformation and is helpful to them. Leonardo believes that there has been an eruption of God in Latin America, and that God has honoured the poor with his sacrament of self-communication.

THE LIBERATION OF SPIRITUALITY

These few examples suffice to show that spirituality itself has to pass through liberation so as to be recast freely on the new perspective and reality of the renewing work of God in the world and in the Church. It must experience its own liberation from the models which were good in other places and in other times, but which may prove to be neither relevant nor faithful in another place and time, as for instance, in Latin America today. Such a liberation is necessary for apprehending the signs of renewal and for experiencing the foretaste of the new creation. The new Anglican Prayer Books indicate this direction through the variations and by means of the flexibility with which they provide more participative worship in their translation and celebration of God's mystery. Their more dynamic understanding of the liturgy provides us with the minimum necessary framework for new experience and experimentation, so that worship does not fall into a kind of enchantment of the worshippers with themselves and occasion the loss of fundamental objective memory and tradition.

The conventional understanding of prayer also needs some revision. In the traditional dictum *ora et labora* work acquires its meaning and gets its sanctification as the prolongation of prayer. On the contrary, L. Boff argues,[21] work has meaning on its own, when done rightly for the building up of the earthly city as God wills as a foretaste of the heavenly city. Especially, work for justice in commitment to poor and oppressed people turns out as what every prayer is meant to be, namely, meeting God. Liturgy has an *intensive* form, enacted when Christians come together, and an *extensive* form enacted when the community scatters.[22] So prayer and action belong together and enrich each other mutually.

THE PRIMACY OF ACTION

The emphasis of action over words found among those who are engaged in the liberation movement is understandable. The Lambeth Conference of 1968 and 1978 showed a certain understanding of revolutionary ferment in the Third World, a line of thinking which insists on the fact that spiritual renewal implies equal concern for the structural transformation of society.

There is indeed an extremist version of the emphasis on action, one which evaluates spirituality exclusively in the light of revolutionary militancy. The model of society which is sought is a socialist one. Any other formulation than that worked out in the experience of militancy is considered oppressive idolatry. This view is a challenge, because it is true that the worship and the glorification of God have to do with the realisation of his justice, and because reconciliation must never be an easy harmonisation which hides the real problem. Nevertheless, a true grasp of the iconoclastic and reconstructive work of God must have a place within any movement of renewal or revolutionary militancy, lest we fall into the temptation of equating some historical project with the Kingdom of God.[23]

The vision of the Kingdom of final liberation enables any liberation or renewal now to be kept open for continual renewal in this time before the last times. In the life of the Church this means a commitment to renewal in faith, liturgy, ministry, mission, structure, and ecumenical dialogue as was suggested by Lambeth 1968. Spirituality that engages in the transformation of society needs continuous reflection and renewal lest the vision of the ultimate goal be lost in myopic narrowness and astigmatic distortion.

RENEWAL IN THEOLOGY

The Lambeth Conference of 1968 indicated the Church's perception that renewal is also required in the field of theology. Renewal does not come to exhortation nor by reiteration of traditional phrases. It is necessary that the Word be understood primarily as Christ witnessed to in the Bible, and also in action in the world which surrounds us. This is a matter of the nature of faith, whether it is trustful relationship or knowledge.

The critical study of the Bible – the Old Testament as well as the New Testament – is vitally related to renewal. Here it is worth observing that renewal in the Roman Catholic Church in Brazil, particularly in the Archdiocese of São Paulo, in the National Conference of Bishops, and in publications, is due in great part to renewal in biblical studies, which show a kind of exegesis freed from dogmatic concern.

Theology needs liberation from past issues which had meaning in other times and other places, but which do not represent real issues in our place and in our time. It needs to be freed from the approach that what faith talks about can be defined, controlled, and even possessed. Theology may speak in parabolic, imaginative and poetic language, with a savour of compassion, so as to evoke faithful, reliable and trustful relationship. Rubem Alves says that the function of the theologian is to be a server of the aperitif of truth. Spiritual renewal also demands sharing theological resources among the poorer Provinces, as was suggested by the pre-Lambeth Conference held at Huampani, Lima, Peru, in early 1986.

RENEWAL AND THE EUCHARIST

The Eucharist is the most powerful source of, and exercise in, spirituality for renewal, because it focuses all the components considered so far. It is the gathering of God's people in order to share before him and with one another that one story which comprehends so widely and so deeply the joy of praise as well as the cry for help of all sorts and kinds of people in their diverse conditions of life as so powerfully summed up, lived, and fulfilled in the birth, life, death and resurrection of Jesus.

The spirituality of which the eucharist is a source and exercise is one which leads toward the renewal of humanity. Eating and drinking are so deeply and vitally related with praise, thanksgiving and supplication that their suppression would imply the confinement of the Holy Spirit in some corner of life – a kind of confession that this life, and this world that God so loved, are not redeemable and sanctifiable. Eating and drinking may also point us to an outward view, namely, the hunger of the world as the absence of true human community. The area in which people are distressed seems to be a suitable location for the Risen Lord to be proclaimed, celebrated and served.

RENEWAL AND CONCERN WITH ECUMENICITY

At Lambeth 1968 there was a slight yet meaningful change in the concept of unity. 'We find ourselves impelled – but gladly impelled – to think first of the world. Its divisions clamour for healing and we see God's purpose for its unity as a cause even more urgent than the unity of the Church'. This change has at least two implications for the ecumenical dialogue: first, talk cannot be restricted to questions concerning doctrines and order. The problem of divisions in the world turns around powerful and powerless nations, and within any system and everywhere a participatory life is a demand. Secondly, the unity of the Church has to be an eschatological sign of the new creation. Therefore, for instance, a practice which cannot include ordained women or allow baptised children at the Lord's Table gives a sign which is defective and a betrayal of the inclusive unity of the Church.

Renewal spirituality must take seriously the silence or similar sanctions imposed on theologians like Hans Küng, Leonardo Boff, and others by the official authority of their church. Their marginal- isation is an ecumenical challenge to pursue clarification on points that were apparently clear, yet have been shown to be not so clear as was supposed. The fact that these theologians hold an ecclesiology sympathetic to many Anglicans raises a serious question.

For Provinces where Anglicans are a minority, the sense of belonging to a world-wide family is an important component for a spirituality concerned with ecumenism and renewal. These minorities need liberation from a minority complex. Where we are a minority, we can also learn that a clear view of God's purpose matters more than the size of the Churches participating in the dialogue. This means that inter-Anglican co-operation on ecumenical matters and on theological education becomes important. The implications of 'dispersed authority' in all realms of the Church's life and mission should be worked out mutually. For example, studies at the parish level of the rites of Baptism and Confirmation, the Ordinals, and the Eucharist, together with contemporary biblical studies, are desirable and necessary. Of course, such study should be turned outward to mission and to the oppressed, or it will not be renewal at all.

NOTES

[1] Eucharistic Prayer B in the American Book and Eucharistic Prayer 3 in the Canadian Book. Oração Eucharistica alternative B do Rito II, de Igreja Episcopal do Brasil.

[2] Walter, Altmann, "The Renewal of Commitment" in *A Vocação Com- prometida com o Reino* (Report of the Preparatory Meeting for Latin American Council of Churches) São Paulo, Imprensa Metodista, 1982, p. 22.

[3] G. W. H. Lampe, *God as Spirit,* SCM Press, pp. 177, 178.

[4] J. Moltmann, *The Trinity and Kingdom,* p. 126.

[5] Pablo Richard, Severino Croato, and Jorge Pixley, *A Luta dos Deuses* S. Paulo: Edições Paulinas, 1985.

[6] *Old Testament Theology,* Vol. I, p. 219. Von Rad says also that the intention of 'the commandment forbidding images was not by any means

to debar the people of Israel from representing Jahweh in concrete form – as a matter of fact Jahweh was always thought of as having human form, like that of a man' (p. 219).

[7] *Teologia do Cativeiro e da Libertação.* Petropolis: Editora Vozes, 1980, pp. 123-24. Walter Brueggemann in his *The Bible Makes Sense* develops the Biblical Covenantal Model in contrast to the Modern-Industrial-Scientific Model and Existentialist Model. In his criticism of the Scientific Model, Brueggemann singles out the notion 'that knowledge is power and, therefore, that life consists in acquiring enough knowledge to control and predict our world, and thereby to secure our own life against danger and threat'. He continues to say 'such an understanding of reality places a high value on competence and achieving, on success and getting ahead'.

[8] *Op. cit.,* pp. 259-61.

[9] *The Lambeth Conference 1968,* SPCK, p. 81. See also p. 72.

[10] *Violência, Povo e Policia* S. Paulo: Editora Brasiliense, 1983. It is interesting to see that 'the violence that the Old Testament condemns in concrete form', according to Thomas Hanks, 'is the institutionalised violence on the part of rich oppressor. The force with which the poor and oppressed defend themselves never merits the Bible's condemnation, nor is it called "violence"'. *God So Loved the Third World,* Orbis Books 1983, p. 106.

[11] *L Fuerza Historica de los Pobres,* p. 204.

[12] The authors of *Anglican Spirituality* edited by William J. Wolf remind us that Anglican spirituality is ecclesiastical, social, holistic and incarnational, the Prayer Book being a co-ordination of many spiritualities. Also the authors tells us that Anglican spirituality is the application in both personal and social existence of the principle of freedom, fellowship and service as derived from the purpose of God revealed in Christ in sacrificial love.

[13] G. Gutierrez, *We Drink From Our Own Wells,* (cf. L. Boff, *Life According to the Spirit:* what gives life to practice and theory of liberation is the spiritual experience of meeting the Lord in the poor.

[14] The appendix was elaborated at the request of the Roman Catholic Archdiocese of São Paulo.

[15] Quoted by L. Boff in *Teologia do Cativeiro e da Libertação,* p. 22; also in Mnika Hellwig, *The Eucharist and the Hunger of the World,* p. 51.

[16] P. Richard, *The Material Basis for Spirituality,* Estudos Biblicos/ Petrópolivoves, 1985; L. Boff in many of his works; G. Gutierrez, op. cit.; J. C. Maraschin, 'Fragmentos das Harminias e Dissonâncias do Corpo' in *Estudos de Religiao* No. 1, May 1985, pp. 193-213.

[17] *Liberation Theology*, pp. 261ff.

[18] G. Gutierrez, *We Drink from Our Own Wells*.

[19] *Life According to the Spirit*, chapter on 'Mystics on politics – contemplation in the Liberation'.

[20] W. Brueggemann, *The Prophetic Imagination*.

[21] *Life According to the Spirit*.

[22] *Liturgy for Living*, p. 23.

[23] Paul L. Lehmann in his *The Transfiguration of Politics: The Presence and Power of Jesus of Nazareth in and over Human Affairs*, Harper & Row, 1975, has a section on 'Beyond Iconoclasm and Idolatry', worthy of meditation on not being blind to the idols inside when the iconoclastic protest against idols is directed outwards.

9

The Contribution of Women to the Renewal of the Church

Grace W. Gitari

In the Anglican Church, as in other churches, considerably more than half the members are women. It is appropriate therefore to consider what special problems and opportunities women may have as they make their contribution to the Church's renewal.

I am grateful that as the person invited to reflect on this theme I will be fairly representative of the views of women in one of the fastest-growing areas of Anglicanism in the world.[1] It is well known that the numerical strength of Anglicanism has moved away from its traditional strongholds in Britain and North America, and that it is in the countries of the Third World that the majority of Anglicans can now be found. I have therefore made a conscious effort to speak always from the perspective of my own culture and background, since that perspective is one of which the whole Church needs to be aware.

I am a Kenyan. I write as a woman born, raised and married in Kenya. The life of women in the homes and villages, in the towns and markets of our land, is well-known to me. My perceptions have also been shaped by the experience of serving for the past eleven years as the Chairperson of the Mothers' Union in our diocese, the Diocese of Mount Kenya East.[2] During that period I have also had the privilege of attending a number of international conferences and gatherings at which I have learned something of the condition of women in the Church at large. These wider contacts have helped me to recognise areas where our East African viewpoint may serve as a fresh insight, or a corrective – or even a recall to biblical standards – to the Church at large.

My own standpoint, like that of so many of my sisters in East Africa, is that of one who knows the reality of Jesus Christ as her personal saviour. Since my encounter with the risen Lord my life has been transformed; and in my ministry among women I have known him as a friend, a comforter, a victor and the source of all the strength I need.

WOMEN IN RENEWAL

In our country, Revival and Renewal mean two very different spiritual movements within the Church in which women have had a significant role. In about 1922 the first conversions took place in Rwanda, later followed by conversions in Uganda and then with gathering momentum in Tanganyika (Tanzania) and in Kenya, in what came to be called the East African Revival Movement. The movement's beginnings in Kenya were in about 1936; by the 1950s it was a force to be reckoned with and was a pillar of strength to many Christians, especially during the Mau Mau war of 1952-60. Moving testimony to the courage of Christians at that time can be found in St James and All Martyrs Memorial Cathedral in Murang'a (formerly Fort Hall). The walls of the cathedral are covered with a series of mural paintings which recall both the Lord's life and ministry, and also the sufferings of his servants, both men and women, who suffered death rather than deny him at the time of the Kenyan Emergency.

The movement lays stress on evangelism, concentrating on conversion (accepting the Lord Jesus as Lord and personal saviour), confession of sin and making a complete about-turn in life. This is a historic occurrence in a person's life; in most cases it takes place in a specific year, on a specific day. Those who are saved concentrate more on their journey to heaven than on worldly matters. Though the movement is very legalistic, with many do's and don'ts for women (which makes it very difficult for modern youth to fit into), it has been a real blessing within the Church. Those who have been saved through this movement, with few exceptions, become firmly rooted and find it hard to turn back from their Christian faith.

In the 1960s the Renewal (Charismatic) Movement made its appearance and remained very strong throughout the 1970s. It was expressed in an uninhibited manner of prayer, with great emphasis on speaking in tongues and on Baptism by immersion. It attracted many young people, including many Anglicans, especially in schools. The Anglican Church lost a lot of its young people this way, and was made aware that there was a great need for a teaching ministry, especially concerning the validity of Baptism with a little water as opposed to full immersion in rivers, and also concerning what the Bible has to say about spiritual gifts and how to exercise them. The Anglican Church was also faced with the problem of how to marry the free expression of the Charismatic Movement with the traditional, formal service without sacrificing what was best in either.

These two movements have had a lot to do with our work. Many older women have fitted comfortably within the Revival movement and the formal Anglican tradition. Those in their forties are the children of the transition, having grown up under the strong influence of the Revival while also encountering renewal in the Charismatic Movement. The younger generation now seems freer to choose where they fit in. Nevertheless the younger woman, generally educated, who does not want to be restricted by the regulations of the Revival Movement and who is attracted by the Charismatics, is in an awkward position, although some will remain true Anglicans. But all of them need to express both the joy of their salvation and the gifts God has given them.

A need has arisen for a ministry of reconciliation between the two movements. After the formal service, or at other times, the congregations divide into groups. The Revival Brethren meet on their own; those with Charismatic leanings do likewise. However the MU, which is not a doctrinal grouping but a women's organisation within the Anglican Communion, has room for both. The participants' real joy is not seen until, the formal meeting finished, they join in singing and dancing outside the church building. Few are the men who will join in such singing, yet the few who do are infected by their joy! This is the high point of our meetings.

Both movements have done tremendous work through their evangelistic conventions and crusades and have been a real blessing to the Church, and many souls have been saved in spite of the problems that arise out of doctrinal differences. We are happy that within the MU we are able to preserve the best of both.

WOMEN AND CULTURE

To work among women is to be placed among that half of the world's residents which is beset with problems of all shapes and sizes. I believe *all* women in *all* cultures suffer, the only difference being the various degrees to which each culture subjects its own women to these problems according to tradition and beliefs. During international conferences we have discussed women's problems and children's problems; and once you touch women and children you automatically drag in men's problems and society's problems too. To work among women, therefore, is to touch on every aspect of personal and family life, because of the extent to which the society they live in influences them. This truth is no respecter of colour, creed, tradition or society.

During the Lambeth Conference in 1978, Dr Dominian, a psychologist and expert on marriage counselling, spoke to the Bishops' wives on their own. He said much that helped many, I believe, concerning human development and what problems are encountered at what stages and ages, especially in marriage; and the talk was greatly appreciated. But after the talk there was a question session. One lady asked: 'Dr Dominian, you have spoken to us and told us all these good things. Do you tell these things to our men too?' This was a revealing question from someone from a different culture from mine. It is true even in the 'Church culture' that much good teaching is given which is appreciated by the women who form the great majority in almost every church. But to have a 'total' society we need 'total' women and 'total' men too. In the following sections we shall refer to women, their needs and strengths: but it would be a mistake to think that we can treat women in isolation. Our concern is with women in the place which society gives them. Renewal of the Church must include renewal in the relationships between men and women, within the family and in their partnership in the Church as well as in Society, so that both may enter more fully into the freedom that is in Christ.

WOMEN AND THEIR PROBLEMS

(a) *Physiological*

The importance of women's physical make-up is, strangely, often underestimated by men. Puberty and adolescence introduce women to physical problems which continue until the end of their days. There is the monthly shedding of blood, easier for some than for others; the agony of childbearing, problems of middle age and finally menopause, bringing with it peculiar problems, diseases and ailments. This may make their life sound bleak and weak, but they are blessed with tough endurance that withstands much physical pain and psychological strain. Of course the majority of women accept it as natural and normal and thus halve the impact of their discomforts. I have heard some wives comment with a light touch that when their husbands are ill they are more delicate to handle than their offspring!

(b) *Marriage*

The most sensitive area in working among women is marriage. There are many forces working against a marriage union – the traditional view of women, the current trends, the misconceptions of individuals, cultures and societies, and the expectations of those who enter into it. Perhaps one of the most serious of all is the war between the 'home-makers' and the 'home-breakers'; they are found in every society. The home-breakers may be acting deliberately with the intent of causing pain or they may be induced to act thus by men or by circumstances.

Three of the many misconceptions in our society that cause great concern are that no man should sleep with only one woman; that cheating in marriage is fine as long as one is not found out; and that no man should listen to a woman's advice unless, as in the case of Thomas, there is no escape from the conclusion that she is right beyond any possibility of doubt. Most women agree that if only husbands took time to listen, they would avoid catastrophes both for themselves and their families. Instead, discussions between husband and wife are usually seen as putting the masculine ego 'on the line'. The wife's opinions are dismissed, even at the cost of shipwreck for the man and his family.

In my culture many wives are accused of sending their spouses wandering because of 'nagging', constantly demanding to know where the husband has been and who he has been seeing. But no wife nags unless there is reason to suspect that her husband is treating his marriage vows lightly; and unfortunately the majority of wives who nag are right in this belief.

(c) *The Church*

Some sections of the Church are caught up in moral decay and sexual permissiveness. The result is that women may fail to find support when they most need it and from the quarter where they have most right to expect it. Dr Billy Graham could have been speaking for Christian women in East Africa when he wrote:

> In many churches one can attend services for a full year without once hearing the word 'sin' mentioned. Not a few leaders of religion have fallen prey to this permissive thinking which holds that there are no absolutes, that the right or wrong of an act depends upon the circumstances of time and place. As for such acts of premarital and extramarital sex, these are said to be justified 'if the relationship is meaningful' and 'if it hurts nobody else'. With even religious leaders talking this way, it is small wonder that the youth is bewildered, and that the Church's moral authority is eroding almost to vanishing point ... Amid our shifting moral standards, the commandment 'you shall not commit adultery' stands as firm today as when God wrote it on tablets of stone ... Sexual sin can only make the strong weak, the wise foolish, and the great ordinary.'[3]

The Bible is full of examples, and does not spare anyone, great or small, in describing their sin and its tragic consequences. Though God forgives, the ugly scars of this sin linger long in life and one has to bear the consequences.

What is the impact on women who take marriage in all seriousness when a spouse commits adultery, irrespective of the degree of involvement? (This does not by any means imply that there are no wives who commit adultery too.) Describe it as an *emotional accident.* Just as one gets hit physically by a car and sustains fractures and injuries, so an emotionally hit person sustains fractures to the heart and soul. The weaker will break down mentally, the majority will sustain injuries which will take long to heal and leave ugly scars, some will quit the marriage, and only a very few will 'take it in their stride'. Those who have been cheated describe shock, disbelief and heartbreak, and a feeling of nakedness which no amount or cost of clothes can cover, the reason being that what was once private and special becomes exposed and public. Women will struggle to put up with this kind of humiliation to protect their children, but the children still get hurt.

(d) *Fundamental Rights and Freedoms*

In the preparatory documents for our recent diocesan synod, the Bishop added this paragraph to the MU's five-year priorities:

> *Fundamental Rights and Freedoms* Women are often victims of unnecessary exploitation. (Our priority is to) teach women the fundamental human rights and freedoms as contained in the Constitution of Kenya (and to) encourage women to participate in the decision-making processes of the community.

During the Non-Governmental Organisations (NGO) Forum '85 held in Nairobi in connection with the United Nations Decade of Women, we attended a session on the exploitation of female sexuality. We each received slips of paper on which had been written at the dictation of those present all the 'horrible' things that men used to exploit female sexuality, such as pornography, advertisements, rape, sex for hire, unequal pay for equal work ... the list was endless We were asked to destroy the lists and throw them away. We were then asked to suggest all the good things that we would demand that men do to us. As the list was being written, a very interesting thing happened. There was a sudden departure of many from the session. Why? Because it was just a swing from one side of the scales to the other. The participants were demanding from men all the things men were exploiting them with, and which they were not complaining about. What then is the answer?

In one television news item recently the Archbishop of Cape Town, the Most Reverend Desmond Tutu, addressed a mixed congregation in the church with these words: 'We will be free, but we can only be free *together.*' I felt that these words summarised what could be the answer to a marriage relationship, that we too can only be free together. When one seeks more freedom at the expense of the other in any relationship, the balance is lost and is replaced by trouble.

THE INDIVIDUAL WOMAN IN SOCIETY

As I have walked along the road, shopped in the market, visited the shops in our streets and travelled in buses and communal taxis, I have listened and heard women's problems. Questions during seminars reveal how grave some of the problems are. It seems, negatively, that it is all 'toil and trouble'. For example, two young women carrying their babies on their backs as they walked along discussed as follows: 'If God gave you a beast for a husband, what would you do?' asked one. 'I think you should take care of your beast because God understands', answered her companion. A question in one seminar went like this: 'What do you do if God gives you a chicken of a husband?' The answer: 'The chicken is still yours!' Some questions are unprintable, but all the time Church and society pressurise the women to put up with their impossible situations, while some sections of the Church baptise sin and call it 'weakness'. The Bible is forthright in condemning sin and declaring that all sin will be punished.

About three weeks ago on my way to market I witnessed a woman with a mental breakdown stretch herself on the muddy ground in front of a moving lorry, so that it could crush her. Fortunately she escaped injury. Later she wandered into our home and asked for some food to eat. She was surprised that despite her muddy appearance we talked to her and gave her food. She spoke of how much she loved Jesus and spent much time kneeling and expressing in prayer the fear that, should she renounce her faith, God might wipe her from the face of the earth. It was touching to see how calm she became and what a smile she could give just because someone had shown love to her. When she discovered that we cared, we became her 'prisoners' for six hours. Her major problem? Childlessness and later being thrown out by her husband. Another woman committed suicide when she learned of her husband's incest with their daughter; another cut the throats of her three children and then hanged herself because her husband was having an affair. Both within and outside the Church, society has stressed that the woman must hold the family together, irrespective of the size of the problem or the character of the man; she is really, as long as she can hold on, the burden bearer.

And what a burden it can be! A man brings a strange woman into the marriage bed to humiliate the wife. There is for ever the lurking fear of polygamy in spite of a Church wedding. There are, of course, a lucky few who make good couples and happy families; but the woman's responsibilities do not end. In our culture, in the majority of cases, if the daughters of a family do not turn out as expected, the wife is blamed for failing to give them proper instruction and held responsible for their disgrace. These are the kind of pressures faced by the women who form our society and Church communities.

Endurance is a commendable virtue, but if there comes a point at which even a committed Christian breaks under the yoke of the burden, tormented by unnecessary guilt that they have made their families fail, then there is something terribly wrong that needs correction. There is comfort in the assurance that God will judge everyone individually and everyone will be punished for their own guilt; as Ezek. 33.20 says, 'O house of Israel, I will judge each one of you according to his ways.' One of our proverbs says that people should be carried with banana fibres and not with a rope. This means that one must not carry another in one's heart like a burden on a rope, but lightly as with banana fibres which are very light and easily breakable, so that if they become too heavy a burden their weight will break the fibre and you will be free. Sometimes I am forced by my convictions to tell the women 'Let go before you break!' Just as men have to adjust themselves to the idea that they can be themselves without acting like small gods or supermen, so women have to adjust to the fact that they can be themselves without having to bear the guilt of other people's self-inflicted burdens imposed upon them. In present society, women seem to bear the sole responsibility for the family's well-being, although they exercise no control over the conduct of their husbands. Renewal, then, must include a sharing of the burdens of the family by men and women together. There is no lack of teaching in the Church about women's responsibilities in their families; the men's share also needs to be taught.[4]

CLERGY WIVES

During one of the clergy wives' seminars, one of them said to me: 'I wish you could come to our home and pray and cast out the demons from our house.' This must sound a shocking request to an ordinary lay Christian, but it is not an isolated case. Paul in his advice to Timothy in 1 Tim. 3.1-13 concerning clergy from bishop to deacon wrote:

> If anyone aspires to the office of bishop, he desires a noble task. Now a bishop must be above reproach, the husband of one wife, temperate, sensible, dignified, hospitable, an apt teacher, no drunkard, not violent but gentle, not quarrelsome, and no lover of money. He must manage his own household well, keeping his children submissive and respectful in every way; for if a man does not know how to manage his own household, how can he care for God's church? He must not be a recent

convert, or he may be puffed up with conceit and fall into the condemnation of the devil. Moreover, he must be well thought of by outsiders, or he may fall into reproach and the snare of the devil.

Deacons likewise must be serious, not double-tongued, not addicted to much wine, not greedy for gain; they must hold the mystery of the faith with a clear conscience. And let them also be tested first; then if they prove themselves blameless let them serve as deacons. The women likewise must be serious, no slanderers, but temperate, faithful in all things. Let deacons be the husband of one wife, and let them manage their households well, for those who serve well as deacons gain a good standing for themselves and also great confidence in the faith which is in Christ Jesus. (RSV)

No one can read these words without trembling because of the extremely high standards set for those who enter the ordained ministry. The 'musts' in this passage have the overtones of the 'thou shalt nots' of the Ten Commandments. The service of ordination to the priesthood brings tears to people's eyes because of the very deep vows that the man has to make. This is the standard of perfection the Bible, the Church and the world expect a clergyman to keep, and anything less dishonours the Lord, the Church and himself. The fact that Paul includes the requirement that he must not be a 'recent convert' implies that ideally the clergyman should be a convert, changed and transformed into Christ-like character in life and holiness. Only then can such a high standard be kept. It therefore means that if a clergyman is married, the wife has to keep the same standard too. Sometimes this does not work for clergymen and their wives. The standard is not always kept and some have fallen short of the mark; a fact reflected in the request from the lady in the seminar. It is biblical truth that when a godly man departs from God's way, and the Spirit of God departs from him, he gets possessed by seven demons and we are told that the state of that man is worse than the first. Some wives of those who have felt like joining the ministry have refused to have anything to do with it. In view of this and to make the ministry easier, would it not be fitting for wives of prospective candidates to give honest opinions concerning their entering into the ministry? This might prevent some difficult situations arising later. Nevertheless, difficulties within the ministry vary from culture to culture and from country to country, and each finds solutions appropriate to that situation.

In view of the fact that a married man is required by the Bible to keep a stable home, perhaps the Church and Christian organisations should take precautions against over-exploiting the time and talents of these men by giving them too many invitations and exposing them to temptation. Just as those who serve the Church are responsible for it, so the Church too is corporately responsible for the welfare of those who serve it.

It is fitting here to make a comment concerning overseas studies. The Church must be commended for its concern in giving its staff the best training available and for providing the funds to make this possible. But the Church must also be sensitive to situations where the separation of husbands and wives, when one partner goes away for study, may endure for as long as three years. Our people hunger and thirst for knowledge and will make great sacrifices for it, but where possible such situations should be avoided. As far as possible, the wife should accompany the husband during his studies.

WOMEN AND POLYGAMY

Polygamy, in which one man has more than one wife, is a difficult subject, and has been discussed in the Christian world for many years, but in *men only* forums which cannot be representative of the suffering that women have to endure in many situations. In Gen. 29.15 – 30.24, the Bible contains an account of a polygamous home; it is not different from other polygamous homes. Jacob, a victim of circumstances and culture, becomes a polygamist against his will. The story provides us with a classic picture of the home of a polygamist. Some of the Hebrew traditions are so similar to ours that this story provides an excellent example.

(a) *For Love of Rachel*

Jacob, in spite of his love for Rachel and his seven years' service as 'dowry', is told when he asks for his wife: 'it is not done so in our country, to give the younger before the first-born'. This has been the case in many cultures until recently. So for love of Rachel he serves seven more years and becomes a polygamist.

In some cultures it is prestigious for a rich man to have many wives.

(b) *The Problems of a Polygamous Home*

(i) For love or childbearing? – Women who are married for any other reason than love display pride for the purpose of hurting those who are married for love. This is especially so if the loved wife, whether married in church or not, is barren. Leah kept on hoping that because she bore children for Jacob, his love would be transferred to her.

(ii)   Jealousy – Rachel was jealous because she bore no children for her husband and was very bitter about it, for she said to Jacob, 'Give me children, or I shall die!' Barren wives of polygamous marriages can react by loving the children of the other wives or by deeply resenting them. Jacob, unlike our men, knew that only God gives life and rebuked Rachel. In our cultures women are blamed if they cannot bear children.

(iii)   Rivalry – How much share does each wife get of her husband? Leah asks, 'Is it a small matter that you have taken away my husband? Would you take away my son's mandrakes also?' For Reuben's mandrakes Rachel allows Leah to sleep with Jacob for a night!

(iv)   Quarrels – Though this story does not narrate quarrels among different units of the family, only a handful of such families would be without noticeable quarrels. In fact, those who have been brought up in such families commonly want nothing to do with polygamy.

Two examples may help us to focus our thinking on this subject. During the NGO Forum '85 a woman of about sixty told us the following story during one of the sessions. She and her husband were married in the late 1930s, and had a church wedding (she had even brought their wedding photograph with her). As they were not well-off, they both worked hard and she devoted her life to her family and their farm. Coffee brought them enough income to build a good stone house and to improve their standard of living. However, as she aged with hard work, her husband took a younger wife. In the process the husband turned their children against her and she was finally thrown out of her home. Her children were threatened that they should have nothing to do with her if they wanted to inherit any of the property. 'Now', she concluded, 'I am old, lonely, homeless and poor'; and she burst into tears, sending a chill into all our hearts.

In another case, a woman's husband took a second wife and moved to another piece of land five miles away. The first wife had a mental breakdown. Now she treks that distance early every morning, scolds her husband, and then treks back again to continue with her business.

As polygamy is something deeply engrained in our men's minds whether they are Christian or not, most wives who have been married in church remain deeply conscious that anything could happen, whether it will be done openly or secretly practised. Whichever way it is done, it hurts very badly and will cause 'emotional accidents' of varying degrees of seriousness.

One of the problems faced by the MU is second and subsequent wives of polygamists who wish to become members. The MU stresses monogamy and Christian family life and does not allow such wives to join the Union. The MU has however welcomed them to join meetings where everyone will be addressed and advised on family matters.

Whatever good may have been said about polygamy in the past, it now remains a threat to monogamy, a heart-, peace- and home-breaker. Happy are the women who have a firm faith in God and have the Lord Christ for a friend, for when the credibility of love and fidelity is shattered they will be sustained.

THE CORPORATE ROLE OF WOMEN IN THE CHURCH

It is noticeable that whenever there is a spiritually strong group of women in a parish, the strength of that parish can also be felt, especially in carrying out its activities such as entertainment, fundraising for church activities and uplifting the standard of living of women, especially at the village level.

Our diocese sees the Church's role as having four dimensions, summarised in the description of Jesus' human development in Luke 2.52: 'And Jesus increased in wisdom (mental and intellectual development), and stature (physical development), in favour with God (spiritual development) and man (social development).'

This can be stated as a commitment to serve the *whole* man. The practical consequence is large-scale projects in education, community development and health, the spiritual ministry of preaching and teaching, and social development both as a consequence of the pastoral ministry and as a diocesan activity in its own right.

The role of women in this kind of human development, though not obvious at first, is unsurpassed. They provide the very basic beginnings of those dimensions right from the moment a child is born. It is the mother who instils the basic words and ideas of moral, cultural and traditional values into the children before they leave home and join institutions of intellectual knowledge. It is the mother who is concerned about what the family eats and thus determines the physical fitness of her family. It is generally true that the mother has more opportunities for praying or reading and discussing scripture and spiritual values than the father. The love and concern of women for their children, sometimes with endurance under very difficult circumstances, protects at least the majority of children from becoming social misfits. We have therefore a proverb in the Swahili language: 'Asiyefunzwa na mama hufunzwa na ulimwengu', which means that anyone who is not offered or does not heed the advice of his mother will be taught by the world.

With the foregoing in mind, the MU is deeply concerned with the condition of the mother and goes to great lengths to ensure that every women as far as possible is able to play this role properly. To this end seminars, conferences and training sessions are held from diocesan to parish level, to equip as many women as possible with knowledge and understanding of these dimensions and how to carry them out. Where specialised knowledge is needed, those conversant with the subjects are invited to give lectures to the women during training sessions or seminars. We totally agree with the saying that 'If you educate a man you educate an individual; but if you educate a woman you educate a whole family.'

On parish and diocesan special occasions the women busy themselves not only with serving guests but also by entertaining them with singing and traditional dancing. This ministry may contain spiritual messages and challenges, histories of their parish, or praise. In daily life, some women have also joined in self-help groups and initiate projects for their own needs or for the needs of their churches and parishes. It is our hope that by uplifting the standard of individual women we shall consequently uplift the standard of many families, of the Church and of the nation.

WOMEN IN MISSION

The witness to the risen Lord on Easter Day began, according to the synoptic Gospels (Matt. 28.1-10 pars) and John (20.1-18) with the testimony of a woman, Mary Magdalen, from whom Jesus had cast out seven demons. John records only one woman, but the others supply more names. Mark, Luke and John record one very important fact concerning the resurrection, that when these women had been to the tomb early in the morning, had seen and talked with the angels and in Mary's case had actually talked to the Lord, and when they then took the news back to the disciples, the disciples *did not believe them.* Peter and John had to go there and see for themselves, but they saw nothing except the linen cloths. Thomas, the true scientist, wanted some tangible proof of the resurrection. Matthew concentrates on recording the story of the guards and the chief priests and elders, so that the truth of the resurrection may not be watered down by false stories. Matthew also says that even after the Lord had appeared to them in Galilee, *some doubted!* All the synoptics record that only the women *saw* the angels, and only the women were *given* the message to go and tell the disciples to go and meet the Lord in Galilee. The disciples, for fear, were hiding, and some had gone back to their houses.

Whatever may be the theological interpretation of these details, they reveal a deep-rooted spiritual relationship between the Lord and the women who followed him on earth as he preached, taught and performed miracles. They must have taken his words about his resurrection as a fact, and though their faith was 'silent', as it were, it had tremendous impact then and through the centuries. Perhaps this may summarise the nature of women in mission through the centuries and throughout the world. Their ministry is 'silent', for as soon as the question of public ministry arises men and women, Churches and denominations, traditions and cultures part company. The Church world-wide has debated the issue of the ordination of women, but although this remains a problem to many consciences there is no doubt that women make a tremendous contribution to the growth of the Church. Their faith, once grasped, remains a dynamic force in their lives against many odds and is a strength to the Church, for it is generally true that there are more women than men in the Church.

Though women's advice and words, like any others, need to be weighed, full credit must be given to those men who having seen reason and good sense in the testimony and ideas of women, have spared no effort in giving their ideas effect. The resurrection itself is a case in point; once the men had been convinced of that to which the women had testified, they left home and comfort, risked their lives and suffered torture and death for the sake of passing on the eternal message.

Women may perhaps have to be content to continue with their silent ministry for the time being; yet they must fully utilise all the chances they are given to witness to the risen Lord in word, deed, song and service: for to them the resurrection is the centre of their life, faith, prayer and hope, because Christ is risen. Praise his name - AMEN!

NOTES

[1] In the Diocese of Mount Kenya East, for example, church growth of 17.2 per cent was experienced in 1985. This figure refers to adult baptisms as a percentage of worshippers, and is based on returns from two censuses completed by 41 of the diocese's then 60 parishes. The average number of worshippers in the diocese was 31,789. Source: Report from the diocesan statistician (Dr Emil Chandran), Diocesan Synod Preparatory Documents, April 1986.

[2] The MU in Mount Kenya East diocese is an organisation with considerable influence in church life, as may be judged by the enrolment figures (498 new enrolments in 1984; 511 in 1985), and by the figures for internal giving (almost 200,000 Kenya shillings in 1984-5, or $13,000 approx.). We have been greatly assisted by the generosity of MU in England in supporting our two staff workers.

[3] From an article in *Reader's Digest,* August 1970.

[4] The problems of women in their families if the men do not share the burden can be illustrated with an example from our country. We have a fishing bird called Ngune. It mainly catches live frogs from water and brings them on land in the hope that they will dry and be ready for eating. Having caught one it then goes back to look for some more in the water. Of course the frog gets terrified and looks for the fastest escape route back to water. When Ngune comes back for his meal, it has already gone. So, people of this area have coined a phrase — 'Ngune's work'. Though Ngune eats some, the greatest part of his labour is wasted. In our discussions, lectures, seminars on family responsibilities we feel sometimes as if we are doing 'Ngune's work' because only one side is involved.

10

The Role of Religious Communities in Renewal

Vincent Strudwick

Religious Life and Spirituality

I once knew a member of a religious community who had been working in the monastic kitchen for seventeen years. It was not work that was particularly congenial to him, but he did it to the best of his ability. However, he found it increasingly difficult to concentrate in his time of prayer. At last he plucked up courage to go to his Superior[1] and ask to be given another task which might enable him to have time for prayer. When he came out he questioned another brother who was about to go in: 'What does *laborare est orare* mean?' He was given the answer and walked away sadly, shaking his head and saying, 'I was afraid it did'. This incident took place over forty years ago, but in it is contained both something concerning the practice of spirituality[2] that is often experienced and expressed by those living the religious life, and also a glimpse of some attitudes that most religious orders have now shed.

The Emergence of Religious Communities as Expressions of Renewal

Of course there is no one spirituality which can contain and express the inspiration and practice of the great religious orders whose histories span centuries. Religious communities are born when the Church is alive and open to the Holy Spirit and is renewing itself in mission, and they are founded as part of a particular response to the needs and insights of the day. They come into being as a result of crisis. The Benedictines came to birth in a time of great instability when the world was in upheaval following the collapse of the Roman Empire. In a time of change their contribution to spiritual renewal was focused in their stability – stability of place and stability of values in an ever-shifting scene. In the thirteenth century the Friar's spirituality was quite different. Feudalism was giving way to a new and different vision of society. This was based on capitalism and the dominance of a new merchant class following the Crusades and the opening out of the great trade routes to the east. Franciscan spirituality with its emphasis on poverty enabled spiritual growth by allowing those who embraced it to sit lightly, and joyfully lightly, to those things that showed evidence of being the dark side of this new society – self-interest and acquisitiveness. During the Reformation period Ignatius of Loyola founded the Jesuits. Ignatius envisaged a religious life which could experience God in the everyday, in the activity of a busy life.

> One could experience God deeply and joyfully in the anguishing con-
> tradictions, persecutions and humiliations which necessarily accompany an
> active life devoted to apostolate. And so he [Ignatius] spoke constantly
> of the presence of God and of finding God in all things, and he opposed
> those of his companions who wanted to disappear into solitude for years
> in preparation for activity.[3]

The renewal and refounding of religious communities in England in the nineteenth century came about as part of a realisation that the Christian world was in fact becoming detached from its Christian roots and that there was a need to recover the vision of a Christian society. The religious communities signalled the presence of the kingdom of God, not only by being there, but by the way in which their members felt impelled to express the values of the kingdom in social action and protest. Much of the work which was undertaken by the communities was not directly connected with other works of the Church, but was a response to a cry from people in the world, the poor, the sick, orphans and aged: a cry of need, a cry for hope. All these religious communities had their foundation rooted in a gospel call; they had the particular charism and insight of the founder and they were founded as part of a response to the needs of the world as perceived in different generations.

Renewal through the Mixed Life

For some religious[4] the quest for personal holiness has been a dominant part of their vocation and this is an approach that was expressed by a Roman Catholic monk who in the 1960s told the television audience, 'if I didn't think I was going to heaven I wouldn't stay here for three days'.[5] This attitude pervades some of the writings of nineteenth century Anglican religious and can still be detected in the thinking and way of life of members of some communities. It has its roots in a mediaeval tradition that is found in *The Cloud of Unknowing,* which makes a distinction between those called to perfection (these are contemplatives) and those called to salvation (who live an active life). Richard Rolle writes:

> If a man could achieve both lives at once, the contemplative and the active, and sustain and fulfil them, he would be great indeed ... I do not know if anyone has ever done this; it seems to me to be impossible to do both at once.[6]

St Thomas Aquinas, himself a Dominican friar, did not share this view, and commended what he calls 'the mixed life'. This involves sharing the fruits of contemplation with others, and for Aquinas this seemed a better way. He believed 'it was better for the candle to give light than just to burn', and in the same way it was better to share the fruit of contemplation than just to contemplate.

In the nineteenth century revival in the Anglican Church, the mixed life communities proliferated, combining a full choir Office with major educational, medical or social works. These communities managed to sustain the mixed life by running large institutions in which they could construct their own timetables and patterns of work, observing the Church's calendar in a particular way regardless of what was going on outside. When they ventured into the world they often found it difficult to sustain the two lives together without doing damage to one or other of the concepts. For example, some of the Anglican nuns who worked with Florence Nightingale in the Crimea were known as the 'handless angels' because they had a tendency to say Sext (the Midday Office) absolutely on time regardless of whether the wounded were pouring into the hospital or not. More recently an Anglican men's community was faced by what was known within the community as 'the scandal of Terce', when three or four elderly gentlemen were wheeled into the Lady Chapel in order to say the Office for the whole of the Priory – while everyone else got on with their jobs. Many Anglican communities held this tension for over a hundred years, and it is only since 1960 that there has been an appraisal and changes have been made. However, from what has been said it is clear that while Religious may be grouped together as those who are working out their discipleship in a significantly different way from other Christians, each community, society or order varies greatly from the others according to the charism of the founder/foundress, the insights of the Church at the time when they were founded and the perceived needs of the world that their members can address. No community can or should remain the same. The reflective nature of the vocation should ensure that new insights are gained and changes made.

Recent Changes

In the case of nuns the changes have been easily observable. They mark a change that in the Roman Catholic Church has been designated as a move from a 'mixed' life to an 'apostolic' life. Significant changes have been made following the recognition that many religious will work outside the community institution and be involved in shifts, rotas and team work with seculars. This inevitably affects the amount of time spent in the community and the priorities that were once regarded as fixed. Religious are learning a new flexibility which may involve less time in community pursuits but an enhanced quality of membership. Habits have been simplified and shortened, although there has not been the move to Marks and Spencers that has characterised some Roman Catholic congregations.[7] The daily corporate prayer has been greatly simplified, in many cases being cut down to a fourfold Office which has made the attempt to live the mixed life less of a burden and more of a refreshment. This has been necessary because many of the large institutions in which sisters and brothers used to work – schools, hospitals, seminaries such as Kelham and Mirfield, or just large Mother Houses – have been abandoned, and members of communities are living in smaller houses doing work that is related to the everyday of modern life. In these houses it is no longer possible to keep a cloister around a time-table that is different from those of the people with whom one is living and working. Constitutions have been rewritten and Rules simplified. Perhaps most important of all to many elderly as well as young religious, it is now possible to have open, expressive, real relationships with other brothers or sisters within the community and there has been a growth in the quality of the personal life of religious which owes a good deal to the insights of modern psychology, the personal growth movement, and an exploration of the ways in which the insights and disciplines of the spiritual life can be linked with the insights of the social sciences. For most religious, obedience is no longer sought through a blind following of a 'superior' who makes all decisions. 'Mother has a whim of iron', I was once told by a sister. Communities in which this can be said must now be very few indeed.

In the Roman Catholic Church and especially in the Americas, the change has gone even deeper, involving members of communities in political activism and protest, from marches against the Vietnam war to participation in guerrilla groups in Latin American countries. The brotherhoods and sisterhoods of the Church of England have been largely untouched by this kind of radicalisation, yet it has been an *essential part* of the development of Roman Catholic communities with international membership.

Struggle and Questioning

Nevertheless, in the Anglican Communion generally and even in the Church of England, what has characterised the last quarter of a century for most religious is a sense of struggle. In my recent research project on the religious life (1985) and in conversations with many religious of different communities, I made the following list of questions concerning renewal that members are asking themselves. This questioning follows a painful period of reflection on what has happened to them: few novices entering and members leaving; the loss of a sense of security; the loss of long-established work; the risk of exploring personal relationships and the opportunity for renewal in worship and work. Their present questioning is part of the struggle to discern how they and their communities should be developing. The questioning reflects not only the needs of religious but the uncertainties of our society at large and the sense of crisis that hangs over it. The Chinese have two symbols that stand for crisis: one speaks of disaster, and the other of opportunity. I found both these elements present in the questioning and struggle of religious communities.

Personal Questions

How do senior members of the community cope with the loss of institutional roles?

How can new and young entrants be helped to adjust to, and prepare for, a life of poverty, chastity and obedience, and how should these be interpreted?

How do younger members of the community cope with an institution run by Grandmothers (or Grandfathers)? How do religious learn to cope better with pain and loneliness?

Institutional Questions

How can leadership roles be diversified and the management of community affairs modernised while enabling members to remain faithful to the monastic spirit and the charism of the community?

How can we respond to expectations of professional training by new entrants?

How can new and appropriate life-styles be pioneered?

What have the traditional religious communities and new basic communities to offer each other?

Missionary Questions

Who are the poor to whom the Gospel is preached and how can members of communities identify with the poor?

How can religious communities re-interpret the mixed life for today and tomorrow?

How far does an increasingly organisational relationship with the institutional Church blunt the contribution of religious to 'kingdom spotting' in the world?

What is basic to the religious life and what is part of cultural ephemera?[8]

There are many Anglican religious today – not the lunatic fringe – who are questioning the permanence of vows, the traditional safeguards of the lifestyle and the nature of the worship that has traditionally been seen as the *esse* of the religious life. Ten years ago, Fr Anthony Damron OSB, then Prior of the (Anglican) Benedictine community at Three Rivers, Michigan, wrote:

Is it true that life vows are invariably a source of strength for one's growth in the religious life? Are they for everyone who belongs in that vocation? ... These elements are not really basically essential to the monastic life. *To live according to the Gospel, that is the point, the whole point.*[9]

Behind these very immediate questions lies a much more fundamental one that religious have been asking themselves, and that is, what is it all for? Why am I here? Where do I fit in to what God is doing in his world?

New Insights about Mission

Forty years ago Bonhoeffer defined the Gospel task in terms of bridging the enormous gap between the Church and the secular world; of discovering what faith means for modern man without making him 'religious' or 'churchy'; of asking 'what does God mean for people today?' This task still stretches before us like a vast uncharted sea, and one reason for our lack of progress is that the Church has not provided the leadership and theological training that are needed for the task. Why is this?

One inhibiting factor in this failure has been the radically differing interpretations of the nature of the Church and of the task of mission within the Christian community itself. In one view, a clear boundary is maintained between the Church, the body of those who have accepted Jesus as Lord, and the rest of humanity; whatever service is done for humanity in the name of Jesus, the overriding aim is always to win individuals for Christ. As one missionary leader put it, the ultimate criterion for all Christian work must be 'has it won disciples?' The work of the kingdom will be advanced through the growth of the Church, and fostering this growth must therefore be an important priority, in all parts of the world. The contrasting view places the emphasis on the Church as the agent of God's love for the world. Like its Master, the Church exists to serve others in showing God's love. Since it is God's will that all men should be fully human, then the priorities for the Church are set by the state of man in the world of today: wherever men are threatened by inhumanity, that is where God's saving love must be acted out and proclaimed, without looking for any immediate response on the part of the oppressed. The missionary is 'kingdom spotting', that is, attempting to discern what God is up to in a particular place, and joining with him in doing it. In practice, of course, these views may overlap, but this tension needs to be fully acknowledged and explored before any programme can be implemented which will involve the whole people of God. While it would be wrong to overplay the divisions within the Church, to ignore these tensions invites failure.

Back to Basics

The questioning of their vocation by members of religious communities is being done against this ecclesiastical backcloth. It can be argued that what is happening in religious communities is a microcosm of what is happening in the institutional Church at large. The struggle and questioning in communities has forced members back to a radical questioning of their vocation. Which of the views of the Church and of mission seems to spring most often from the religious vocation and life? It is surely that of the Church as the agent of God's love, and this follows from the nature of the religious vocation. This is described by Abhishiktananda[10] in his book *The Further Shore*.[11] He speaks of the Hindu *sannyasis* (monks) as 'essentially acosmic just as were the original Christian monks'. He goes on to say that if this is not understood, then it is impossible to recognise either the essential commitment of the religious or the complete freedom that he or she enjoys. Today 'there is continual pressure on Hindu *sannyasis* here (just as there is on Christian monks in the West) to *do* something or other – whereas in fact the only thing that should be required of them is to *be* in the deepest sense of the word'. At the present juncture in the history of the world, in the east as well as in the west, the sense of mystery is everywhere being increasingly obscured, 'even in those whose special vocation is *to bear witness among their brothers to the eschaton, to the presence here and now of the ultimate realities'.* The spirit of secular activism corrodes everything. So in the west monks and clergy seek to establish their status in society and ask for a social recognition which is purely secular in character. 'In the flood of secularism which is sweeping away all the adventitious sacredness with which their calling was over-laid in previous ages, they lose the sense of their real identity.' This comes out in some communities in the way that some sisters (not always the elderly) oppose changes, especially those that affect the status of the grouping to which they belong. Thus they forget that their primary function is to be the witnesses in the midst of society to what is truly sacred – that which is beyond all forms and definitions. To put it another way, their function is to witness to the kingdom of God and to do so by being, and becoming – and by sharing the fruits of this process. This sharing is done through the gift of discernment, when the signs of the kingdom are seen and encouraged.

The Present Crisis

The witness today is the monastic witness in every age, but in this age the context is one of apocalyptic, because it is now possible to terminate human history, to cease the becoming for ever. Can humanity survive its own destructive powers? Henri Nouwen writes:

> As we reflect on the increasing poverty and hunger, the rapidly spreading hatred and violence within as well as betweeen countries, and the frightening build-up of nuclear weapon systems we come to realise that our world has embarked on a suicidal journey.[12]

The witness to the kingdom of God is a witness which rejects this suicide bid and the madness of the values that make it possible. It is a rejection of 'the world' in this sense, as Thomas Merton, the Roman Catholic Trappist monk, wrote:

> By the monastic life vows, I am saying *no* to all concentration camps, the aerial bombardments, the staged political trials, the judicial murders, the social injustices, the economic tyrannies, and the whole socio-economic apparatus which seems geared for nothing but global destruction in spite of all its fair words in favour of peace. I make monastic silence a protest against the lies of politicians, propagandists and agitators, and when I speak it is to deny that my faith and my church can ever seriously be aligned with these forms of injustice and destruction.[13]

Here is evidence of a radical reappraisal of monastic life in terms of seizing the opportunity that the crisis has provided. 'I make monastic silence a protest ...' Have members of monastic communities in the Anglican Communion similarly seized the opportunity? For the crisis that is shaping the forms of the religious life in this age is similar to, but more radical than, the changes at momentous periods in the past. Of course, as in the past, some communities will die, while others will continue changed, but basically showing continuity with the past. However, some religious now may be joined by others not in vows, seeking to respond to the crisis in new and different ways. As the 1960s saw the radicalisation of individual religious, so the 1990s may see the radicalisation of whole communities if encouragement is given to this process and individuals have the nerve to seize the opportunity.

Domestication versus Renewal

The impetus towards this kind of renewal in the religious communities of the Anglican Communion has been – and may yet continue to be – inhibited by the tendency from both within and without to *domesticate* the communities. In a personal paper a sister in a large community has written:

> I would suggest that once a community has lost its ability altogether to stand on the fringe of the Church, that loss acts as a barometer by which one can measure other losses in that order. There is a universal quality about the religious life – it stretches across traditions and cultures and transcends social status. This is vital especially when in some places the Church becomes associated with specific classes or interest groups.

The process has been complicated and motives have been very mixed, but there is a tendency among some bishops not to be comfortable with Christian institutions which are 'on the fringe' and over which they do not have absolute control. Some religious superiors see in the approval and closer ties with the diocesan bishop a way of ensuring that their community is accepted as a full and proper part of the Church's life and ministry, and this is a legitimate concern. After their meeting at Canterbury in 1982, the Permanent Ecumenical Consultation of Religious issued a statement in which they contrasted the relationship with the Church of Roman Catholic religious as 'integral, even necessary to the Church's full expression' with that of Anglicans who are described as 'few, and less formally incorporated in their Church's structure'. However, in the Roman Catholic Church the freedom of the great international orders from the authority of the local diocesan bishop is a necessary part of the way they function: 'incorporation into the Church's structure' does not imply an obedience to a local bishop. The desire of some English diocesan authorities to exploit the ministerial expertise that is perceived as being 'locked up' in religious communities is understandable. The perception that religious have 'something extra' to offer in the performance of ministerial tasks, coupled with a certain vulnerability in communities with shrinking membership, has led to some disastrous experiments in placing religious in small parochially based houses. Another favourite way for this kind of domestication to occur is when a diocese or other institution invites sisters to run a retreat house without *thinking through* the role that the sisters will fulfil and the structures needed to help them to fulful it.

It is the thinking through of the role that is so vital, for the work of ministry within the Church structure is not *necessarily* domesticating. One large women's community in England quite deliberately decentralised its large mother house in order to create small houses of sisters doing parish work. But they are quite clear about the character of the ministry they offer and the way in which invitations to serve are considered (both by the diocese and by the community) and accepted or rejected. The parish base may provide a springboard for theological discernment and social action.

Perhaps it also needs to be said that a different form of domestication occurs when a community withdraws both from the world and from the Church and becomes wholly preoccupied with preserving the tradition and forms of the religious life and with creating an environment in which the members can live out their lives without reference to Gospel call or Gospel task. 'Preserving the tradition' can be a way by which they are able to maintain a high degree of regularity, comfort and security in their lives. It is a similar preoccupation with preserving the tradition that has inhibited the growth of African novitiates in English-born communities. Conformity to English nineteenth-century middle-class cultural norms, enshrined in the Rule and tradition, has seemed more important than allowing the development within the community of an Africanised interpretation of the founder's charism and the community's Gospel task. One of the few really strong African novitiates in the Anglican Communion belongs to the American Order of the Holy Cross, where both the prior and the novice master of the house in Ghana are Africans and the development of the monastery is based on the acceptance of different cultural insights.

Black Sheep Theology and Ministry

But the real release from the pressures of domestication arises when religious take advantage of their freedom to respond to the crisis and relate to others who are aware of it and searching for meaning. It springs too from that sense of missionary purpose which I described earlier as 'kingdom spotting'.

Monks and nuns attract people's attention. The habit and the romantic way in which people perceive the life is an opportunity which many communities feel it is right to exploit. For through these means members can sometimes touch a few of the many people who are relatively untouched by the Church and its ministry, although in some sense they may still think that they 'belong'. Hence the term 'black sheep'. A 'black sheep' is one who lives else-where and differently but keeps up the family connection in some form, and there is a thread of attachment between the sheep and the folks back at home. This is demonstrated in the present context by very occasional churchgoing (Christmas, perhaps Easter, and some family services), support for the church tower building fund, and a sense of identity which can easily be broken by keen vicars who implement a rigorous baptismal policy or write doctrinaire letters in their parish magazines.

Some years ago I wrote rather critically that 'at a time when education has become increasingly available, the church has with-drawn theology from public debate and concentrated on ministerial training for both clergy and laity, to help them to "be the church better". It is a most important task, but we have come to believe that it is the *only* task of theological education. We need to do more research on the sort of place that people will come to and the sort of atmosphere and goings-on that enable them to cross the threshold. We need more experience in outreach to make the contacts that help people to want to learn and we need more adult theological resource material which is not condescending and not crowded with assumptions and jargon. As it is many people are not being given the opportunity to learn, and theology as an academic discipline is becoming too inward looking. Because of the emphasis on ministerial training, most of the questions are being posed from *within* the church and theology becomes increasingly ecclesiastical and uninteresting to those outside. It is surely when theology is understood and lived in a way that responds to the questions and needs of those outside the church that we can expect the social and cultural climate to change ...'[14]

There is a good deal of evidence to suggest that monasteries and convents are such places, where dialogue can take place and loving pastoral links can be forged, not only with the black sheep but with those beyond the fringe. One American community has estimated that 50,000 people came to the monastery in one year – most of them not church people doing churchy things, but interested and serious black sheep, whose visits ranged from short-stay and contact with one community member, to more sustained and structured dialogues which have been part of the community's programme. Some small houses of English communities have been designed to enable and increase this kind of ministry, whether they are in parishes or whether they are houses such as that run by the sisters of the Order of the Holy Paraclete at Bolgatanga in Ghana, where in the more Muslim north of the country they run low-key social skills programmes for African women and the sisters exercise a personal and wide-ranging ministry. A description of what it feels like to go to a monastery of this kind is given by Pertti Mikael Leiman in his article 'The Mission of a Monastery in present-day Finland'. He writes as one who visited the Orthodox monastery of Valamo, having abandoned Christianity long before:

> Nobody tried to convert me. Having had some experience of charismatic movements in the late '60s which in fact closed the chapter of Christianity for me, I had retained a cautious attitude to any kind of religion. To my surprise and relief, I found an open-minded community where convincing

others was not a way to fortify one's own beliefs. I was allowed to face my preoccupations freely and they were respected as my views.[15]

Leiman finds his experience of living in a community of faith which is open to receive and explore others' insights difficult to describe except metaphorically, but he identifies its effectiveness as being because

> Valamo has retained its old tradition. At the same time it has developed new forms of activity to encounter the present cultural and societal situation in Finland. It has not modernised the long tradition ... Instead it employs a variety of new means to give people an opportunity to 'taste and smell' its spiritual heritage.[16]

'The ministry of hospitality' is on many Chapter agendas, and in those conversations in which I have shared, it has been clear that it is often a development of black sheep ministry that is being sought. It takes many forms, both cerebral and practical, and includes such ventures as Helen House in Oxford – the first hospice for the care of children with life-threatening illness, which began when Mother Frances Dominica of the Society of All Saints invited a sick child to the convent so that her parents could have a much needed rest. It has now developed as a highly specialised venture offering skilled care to the children and their families in a partnership with trained staff. It offers a particular atmosphere of Christian care and Christian inquiry and searching to any whose need leads them there. At the same time, just as those who come to monastic seminars can do so without feeling any pressure upon them to be other than themselves, so families can come to Helen House choosing to receive nothing other than the quality of care and friendship offered. In this project and others, we have evidence of where the questioning has led some communities. Often on the English scene in a *gentle* way, it is nevertheless a developed expression of the same spirituality that in the United States brought Roman Catholic and Episcopalian nuns together in protest against popular values and programmes and in favour of the poor, the underprivileged, the marginal and the suffering; and it is now involving not just individual members but whole communities in a refounding of life and work. To return to Leiman, he proclaims his convictions about the role of a refounded monastery in the following passage:

> The way of life of a monastery is a powerful expression of the idea that faith means practice, that it is not a set of proclaimed beliefs, values and morals. To show this openly is the basic missionary task of the monastery in the present situation.[17]

Apostolic Renewal through the Contemplative Way

The ability of religious to change, and engage in new forms of apostolic ministry, must depend upon the nature and strength of their spiritual life. In his book *Struggle and Fulfilment* Donald Evans describes the contemplative way as:

> the stance of a person who profoundly appreciates the reality and uniqueness of each particular in the universe, including himself. It is fostered by various forms of meditation which discipline his attention, cleanse his vision, and open his heart. Gradually he is liberated from the self-preoccupation and self-consciousness which distort and subjectivize our usual perception of reality. He also becomes aware of a still center within himself which somehow participates in a reality which is ultimate, and from this vantage point, he can see that all things similarly participate.[18]

It is this contemplative way of life which characterises all monastic spirituality. It is the same stance that is described by the author of *The Cloud of Unknowing* in the fourteenth century when he writes:

> There the birth, the life, the suffering, the death, the resurrection of Christ are not merely remembered but inwardly found and enjoyed as a real status of thy soul, which has followed Christ in the regeneration. When once thou art grounded in this inward worship thou wilt have learnt to live unto God above time and place. For every day will be a Sunday to thee, and wherever thou goest thou wilt have a priest, a church and an altar along with thee.[19]

This approach to life and expression of it enables those who are caught up in it to view the world and the Church and their institutions with a certain detachment. There is a deeper reality behind the realities of the everyday, and part of the programme is to perceive and understand what is going on. That is why the true contemplative often and inevitably gets involved in the affairs of the world.

It is this kind of spirituality that has enabled members of some communities, whose numbers have dwindled and whose members are aged, to contemplate the death of both themselves and their communities with equanimity. Their experience is that their particular institution was called into being to serve a certain purpose at a certain time, which has now ended. There is no need to be anxious about perpetuating it, as there is no need to be anxious about perpetuating themselves. It is the same spirituality that has enabled other communities to contemplate radical change – change so momentous that it is hard to conceive.

The Radical Nature of Change in the Religious Life

This kind of change has been described by Paul Collins as a 'mutation'.[20] Father Collins says mutation is a word implying a radical change in the forms and qualities of a given reality; biologically it is the kind of change that results in a new species. 'There is a sense of both disjunction and continuity. Factually there are specific periods in the history of humankind and of the church in which more than "change" is occurring. We are in such a period ...' This is not a new experience for the Church; in fact the first mutation in church history occurred within the New Testament itself, as the Church struggled to disentangle itself from its original Jewish matrix.

The theme is developed by Gerald Arbuckle in an article in *The Tablet*. He lists some 'hard truths' that religious must face if creativity is to emerge from crisis and chaos.

> Most of us were founded to serve the neglected and the poor, but we do our best to hold on to institutions that no longer serve this purpose. Some of us may have a charism that stresses contemplation. We hesitate to revive it, because our active life is so important – or so we believe.[21]

Arbuckle then goes on to say that there must be a refounding of communities: 'we must creatively live out again and again the history of our original founding'. He then says that there must be people of the calibre of refounding persons to lead, and ends with the question 'are we prepared to discover these rather rare people, support them, and respond to their creative leadership?' In the last ten years a number of our Anglican communities have engaged in this process with different results, some positive and some negative. There is still time for more to seize the opportunity of the present crisis for the sake of the Gospel and the Church.

Towards a new Society

It is not just religious observers who are discerning this kind of crisis and change. Alvin Toffler in *The Third Wave*[22] suggests that we are in a period of transition from one civilisation to another. He sees the first of two waves of change as the agricultural revolution, followed by the rise of an industrial civilisation, but suggests that a third wave is now breaking upon us which may bring the death of industrialisation and the rise of a new civilisation. 'The third wave is a genuinely new way of life based on diversified renewable energy resources; on methods of production that make most factory assembly lines obsolete; on non-nuclear families; on a novel institution that might be called "the electronic cottage", and on radically changed schools and corporations of the future.' If we are in such a period of change, what is the Church contributing towards shaping that change? This is where thoughts about renewal should be focused. Bishop Lesslie Newbigin, in *Mission and Evangelism: An Ecumenical Affirmation,* says that

> The Church has lived so long as a permitted and even privileged minority, accepting relegation to the private sphere in a culture whose public life is controlled by a totally different vision of reality, that it has almost lost the power to address a radical challenge to that vision and therefore to modern civilisation as a whole.[23]

In this time of change – radical change – is it not possible that the Church again has an opportunity to address our culture?

If it is to do so, it will not be from a spirituality which is concerned with its own institution, with its own history, and with a care for conservative preservation of what has happened in the past. Nor will it be by attempting to perpetuate what is familiar in the present. The Church of the future will have to be open to make its contribution by drawing on its history and experience, but also on its ability to change creatively. I believe this facility flows from a contemplative and reflective spirituality. If this is renewed, the Church may yet contribute to a changed society, the boundaries of which are undrawn and the content of which has yet to be shaped.

To contribute in this way is not a new idea for monastic spiritual writers. In the twelfth century the Cistercian monk Joachim of Flora wrote of the three ages of man. The third age of which he speaks is 'the age of the Holy Spirit', and in some respects this seems to prefigure much of what Alvin Toffler speaks about in his sociological writings. Is not monastic spirituality one of the keys which will open us to a new understanding of the Spirit and enable his working in us in new ways to open us to radical change in ourselves and our society.

Religious Communities and Renewal

Renewal, where it is taking place in the religious life, is doing so when it is based on a theology of the kingdom, and a concern for the Gospel which overrides any desire of individuals for security and status.

It is taking place in communities of mixed races, where, for example, westernised monastics are being challenged by their African brethren in the way of lifestyle and values; it is taking place where religious are living with other Christians *for the sake of the Gospel* and forging community together; it is taking place where the cloister is no longer a protection for the pious, but a place of opportunity for the enquirer.

Renewal is taking place where questioning and doubt are seen as a necessary part of faith, and where there is a belief in the ability of the community to provide an opportunity for discipleship and a worthwhile tool for mission.

Renewal is taking place where exploration and change are seen as the opportunity that arises from a society in crisis, and to live according to the Gospel is the point, and the whole point.

If these are the areas where renewal is taking place, should not the freedom to explore and change be encouraged by the bishops? Would not a 'Partners in Mission' exercise of religious, in which teams of partners would spent time and share insights, be a way of spreading and hastening the vision of the few across the boundaries of the Anglican Communion? Would not the concept of a 'Mission Audit' assist communities to examine their goals and resources and help the new refounding leaders to emerge with the support of their members? Should we not be excited and confident about the religious life so that we positively encourage people into it as a way of living and changing according to the Gospel?

In effecting their own renewal, religious communities are making both a statement and a contribution to renewal of the Gospel task. If it is true, as is often stated, that 'what happens in the religious communities today, will be experienced by the Church tomorrow', they may also provide a model which can be valuable for the Church as we seek to be renewed through

our understanding of what spirituality means

an audit of Gospel tasks and resources

resisting domestication and concern with our institutional life

questioning and struggle

a concern for the world and an increase in the skills of discernment to discover the kingdom there

a refounding that is both faithful to Gospel and tradition, yet open to change.

It is this last, the ability to explore confidently, that the experience of the religious life seems to call forth. For me its character is focused in the life of Brother Hugh Pearson, who began his life as a religious in Korea at the end of the last century and who was brought home to England when he was nearing ninety after a lifetime of missionary adventure. He refused to rest and, following the pattern of his whole life, began a new exploration. This involved mapping the drainage systems of the large Gilbert Scott house in which the members of his Society lived. It was fun and it was useful, and it satisfied his exploratory instincts. But that too came to an end. When he was dying, the Prior went to him and told him of his state and asked how he felt. 'I'm excited', replied Brother Hugh, looking ahead to the next change, and in that response summed up the essence of monastic spirituality and of the role of the religious communities in renewal.

NOTES

[1] A term still used for 'line management' in Anglican communities, but almost obsolete in the Roman Catholic Church.

[2] One working definition of spirituality is given by Gordon Wakefield in *A Dictionary of Christian Spirituality,* ed. Gordon Wakefield, SCM Press, London 1983. He says that spirituality involves 'those attitudes, beliefs, practices which animate poeple's lives and help them to reach out towards super-sensible realities'.

[3] William Johnston, *The Inner Eye of Love,* Collins, London 1978, p. 25.

[4] A 'religious' is the term used for a member of a religious community.

[5] Geoffrey Moorhouse, *Against All Reason,* Weidenfield & Nicolson, London 1969, facing p. 178. This is an excellent piece of sympathetic investigative journalism researched near the beginning of the recent changes in the religious life. It includes my own research on the training of novices in Anglican communities, prepared for a Downside Symposium, attempting to show that those communities attracting novices were those offering professional training related to the communities' tasks.

[6] Richard Rolle, *The Fire of Love,* tr. Clifton Wolters, Penguin Classics, Harmondsworth 1972, p. 112.

[7] For a personal account of the changes in the Roman Catholic Church, see Prue Wilson, *My Father took me to the Circus.* DLT, London 1984.

[8] Members of many communities are now skilled in the techniques of adult education, and the answers to these questions are being sought through training programmes, using the small group as the basic unit. This kind of training has largely replaced the 'instruction' of former years. Some

communities, as a matter of policy, are doing some of their training together with secular clergy and lay people.

9 Anthony Damron *OSB*, 'Religious Orders: The Order of St Benedict', in *Realities and Visions: The Church's Mission Today*, ed. Furman C. Stough & Urban T. Holmes III, Seabury Press, New York 1976, pp. 122ff. A stimulating discussion of commitment to poverty, chastity and obedience and what it means today is offered by H. A. Williams *CR* in *Poverty, Chastity and Obedience*, Mitchell Beazley, London 1975. Williams too questions the need for life vows (although he has taken them himself) in *Some Day I'll Find You*, Mitchell Beazley, London 1982. 'However certain a man might be in the present that it was God's will he should remain in the community, that present certainty did not qualify him to dictate to God what the divine will must be for the rest of the man's life.' Both CR at Mirfield and SSM at Kelham moved to life vows in the 1930s, having previously been content to express a life *intention*.

10 Abhishiktananda, meaning 'the Anointed One', was the Indian name taken by Henri le Saux, a French Benedictine monk, who completely identified himself with the people of India and lived as one of their own holy men in a hermitage.

11 Abhishiktananda, *The Further Shore*, ISPCK, Delhi 1975.

12 Henri J. M. Nouwen, *The Way of the Heart*, DLT, London 1981.

13 Thomas Merton, *Contemplation in a World of Action*, George Allen & Unwin, London 1971.

14 Vincent Strudwick, quoted in *An Idea Still Working*, Society of the Sacred Mission 1980.

15 Pertti Mikael Leiman, 'The Mission of a Monastery in present day Finland', in *The Ecumenical Review*, January 1986.

16 Ibid.

17 Ibid.

18 Donald Evans, *Struggle and Fulfilment*, Collins, Cleveland 1979.

19 *The Cloud of Unknowing*, tr. Clifton Wolters, Penguin Classics, Harmondsworth 1978.

20 Paul Collins, 'The state of Religious Life today: one man's analysis', in *Review for Religious*, Sept./Oct. 1984.

21 Gerald Arbuckle, 'Out of chaos', in *The Tablet*, 21/28 December 1985.

22 Alvin Toffler, *The Third Wave*, Collins, London 1980.

23 Lesslie Newbigin, in *Mission and Evangelism: An Ecumenical Affirmation*, Conference for World Mission, 1984.

11

Renewal in Past Ages

Gordon S. Wakefield

Renewal is a theme of Holy Scripture. The Lord in bringing his people home from Babylon is doing a new thing. Deutero-Isaiah in proclaiming God's deliverance sees it as in some sense a new creation and fills his oracles with the hope, not to be realised, that this redeeming act will save the world. Ezekiel promises the returned exiles in God's name a new heart; this will change the life of the body politic, but will simultaneously result in the conversion of individuals, henceforth responsible before God (Ezek. 36.26). Jeremiah declares that God will make a new covenant with the house of Israel and the house of Judah, the covenant of divine forgiveness and mercy, the law written, not on tablets of stone, but on each heart, and God known, without admonition, to all (Jer. 31.31ff.)

Christianity itself may be thought of as a renewal movement – new wine in new bottles (Mark 2.22). Its earliest preaching to the adherents of its parent religion announced the fulfilment of the Jewish past but also, through the resurrection, and the gift of the Spirit, its promised end. To a jaded Gentile world it offered hope, a story different from the myths of the immoral, all too human, gods and the cynicism of the philosophers.

There is some evidence that even in New Testament times there were renewal movements within Christianity itself. It is possible to use the seventeenth-century word 'enthusiasm' (Greek *entheos,* in-godded, God-possessed) to describe certain manifestations within the New Testament Church, such as those charismatic outbursts at Corinth which caused trouble to St Paul, and most notably, the Revelation of John. In the latter, the renewal is eschatological. After the woes and the afflictions and the two resurrections:

Then I saw a new heaven and a new earth ... And I saw the holy

139

city, new Jerusalem, coming down out of heaven from God ... And he who sat upon the throne said, 'Behold I make all things new'. (Rev. 21.1-5)

THE NEED OF RENEWAL

Renewal is a principle of a dynamic universe, evidenced in nature, in the cycle of birth, maturity, death and birth again. The biblical theology of grace is thus in harmony with the theology of nature. Newman in his *Essay on Development* wrote, 'In a higher world it is otherwise, but here below to live is to change and to be perfect is to have changed often'.[1] True, he was writing of the 'chronic vigour' of the Catholic Church in its Roman mutation and he thought in terms of continuity of growth and development of doctrine, certainly not of revolutionary, radical changes or of enthusiasm which he deplored and which was contrary to his own temper. Renewal movements are signs of discontinuity, of disturbance, a shaking of the foundations, not of gradual evolution of dogma and discipline but of life out of death. But we may steal Newman's words and tear them from their context to describe what renewal throughout the ages has stood for – change, though radical change, leading to perfection.

It does seem to be a fact of history, as is often observed, that Christianity by its very mission to be in the world and to save the world, sometimes by its very power over human hearts and minds, demands order and institutions and orthodoxy, and then so easily becomes formal, oppressive, perhaps over-intellectualised, so that a new outpouring of the Spirit alone can save it. The treasure is in earthern vessels and we may adapt Jean-Baptiste de Santeüil's hymn about individual apostles and saints to describe what happens to churches:

> Those vessels soon fail, though full of thy light,
> And at thy decree are broken and gone;
> Then brightly appeareth thy truth in its might
> As through the clouds riven the lightnings have shone.

We must not be simplistic here; to trace patterns through history is a difficult task. Renewal movements have indeed begun in reaction to the apathy and atrophy of churches. They then have become organisations themselves, conformist and often equally lacking in *élan vital* with those they disturbed and sought to revive. But renewal has often been spasmodic and has either failed in its main purpose of bringing new life, or in its attempt to halt the all-devouring encroachments of the institution. Methodism began amid the evangelical revivals of the eighteenth century in England. It came almost accidentally to develop into a large world-wide denomination and perhaps the most bureaucratic and inflexible of all the great churches. The nineteenth century saw Methodist renewal movements, some of them in protest against Wesleyan autocracy, all becoming institutionalised by the end of the century. In spite of claims made for the 'Second Evangelical Awakening' which began in Ireland in 1859, there has been no revival within Methodism of more than local and ephemeral effect for at least one hundred and thirty years. It is too early for a historian to assess the influence of the Pentecostal movement of our own time. It has affected all the major denominations, Roman Catholic not least, but not Methodism to the extent of reviving whole Circuits or adding to the membership so as to reverse the melancholy downward trend. We must not at this stage enter into the question of whether social and cultural conditions in the West and North are ripe for a tide of the Spirit which will overcome the barriers of materialism, scepticism and technology. The point is that in an attempt to discern a pattern of renewal we must not ignore these sociological mysteries which may seem to obscure the hand of God; but apart from renewal, there is only death. Order may preserve Christian life and truth; it may embalm it. *Semper reformanda,* always to be reformed, is not so vital a watchword as *semper renovanda,* always to be renewed – for reformation may mean but a change of structure.

A further truism is that renewal may be the consequence of certain truths of the Gospel being neglected in the Church. This is easier to demonstrate. Was not Montanism towards the end of the second century, fanatical and near blasphemous as it was, due in part to a neglect of the doctrine of the Holy Spirit? Was not Franciscanism in the thirteenth century, a movement preserved from heresy and not outlawed by the Church, a devotion to the sacred humanity of Jesus and a recall to stark, literal obedience and the following of the example of him who warned of the dangers of money and had not where to lay his head? And these at a time when Christ was frozen in conventional concepts of his divinity and the Church ever in danger of wealth and worldliness. Not least does renewal spring from the cries of the poor and the oppressed, those submerged by ecclesiastical systems and tyrannised by power-hungry and sometimes unimaginative clerics.

CHARACTERISTICS OF RENEWAL

It is time to turn to certain features which may be discerned in all movements of renewal.

(1) *Power (dunamis)*

'One of the things which connects Fox's *Journal* with the New Testament is the frequency in it of the word power.'[2]

Renewal movements have changed lives, and often by mass conversion. Preaching has been a chief instrument as on the Day of Pentecost according to Acts 2. The preaching has been with power, not the formal discourse, prepared and polished with scholarly allusions, delivered, probably read, in a reverential monotone. There has descended what the Welsh call the *hwyl*. Charles Wesley provides this account of the preaching of Howel Harris, the Welsh enthusiast:

> O what a flame was kindled! Never man spake, in my hearing, as this man spake. What a nursing-father has God sent us! He has indeed learned of the good Shepherd to carry the lambs in his bosom. Such love, such power, such simplicity was irresistible. The lambs dropped down on all sides into their shepherd's arms. Those words broke out like thunder, 'I now find a commission from God to invite all poor sinners, justified or unjustified, to His altar; and I would not for ten thousand worlds be the man that should keep any from it. There I first found Him myself. That is the place of meeting'.[3]

Such scenes were multiplied in the course of the Evangelical Revival, even though John Wesley is said once to have read someone else's sermon in the open air, with consequences by way of paroxysms and conversions similar to when he preached his own. There is here more than the arousing of mass hysteria by a revivalist preacher contriving it by oratorical tricks and counterfeit passion, which Wesley, above all, deplored and sternly discouraged. It is not unlike poetic inspiration, and Geoffrey Nuttall has ventured to compare Harris's preaching with what Sir Maurice Bowra said in his Rede Lectures of 1951, *Inspiration and Poetry*:

> 'The most powerful and most authentic poetry ... creates in us the kind of exaltation which the poet himself has known'; words 'at their best ... communicate something so powerful that it makes us live more

abundantly'. 'We cannot explain how this happens', Sir Maurice says; all he can suggest is that 'inspired words create life in us because they are themselves alive'.[4]

This power was evidenced not only in preaching but in prayer. Renewal movements tend to despise what the Puritans called the 'stinted forms' of prayer books. Even Cranmer's great Litany was thought to be a trifling with God, 'more wishes than prayers'. What they would have thought of so much modern intercession in public worship, which is often little more than a rehearsal of news headlines, can all too easily be imagined. Prayer was an uninhibited outpouring to God, sometimes a wrestling, sometimes a sheer rapture of thanksgiving. Our age will regard it as too verbose, but words, which of themselves were totally inadequate to address God, were the means by which the soul emptied itself that it might be filled with the Divine Spirit.

(2) *Immediacy*

Leaders of renewal were as suspicious of those who forever retold their past experience as they were of those who never moved beyond the bounds of ecclesiastical tradition. The past was dead, and what God had once done in the soul, however marvellous, was no substitute for his living activity here and now. William Berridge of Everton, one of the clergy prominent in the Evangelical Revival, prayed 'that God would give us new bread not stale, but what was baked in the oven on that day'.

Immediacy characterises the Wesley hymns. *Everything that God did in Christ he did for me now.* In his eucharistic doctrine, Wesley is one with the Jewish Passover, with Theodore of Mopsuestia in the fifth century, and with the thought of the twentieth-century Benedictine Dom Odo Casel, when he insists that the Sacrament brings the past into the present, so that what was done once for all on Calvary may be immediately experienced.

> Now let faith pass the years between
> And show thee bleeding on the tree
> My God who dies for me, for me.
>
> Didst thou not in the flesh appear
> And live and die below
> That I may *now* perceive thee near
> And my Redeemer know.
>
> Mercy must not be postponed.

Show me thy salvation *now*.

Speak me in a moment whole.

All things in Christ are ready *now*.

This instant *now* may I receive
  The answer to his powerful prayer.
This instant *now* may I live
  His prevalence with God declare
And soon my spirit in his hands
  Shall stand where my forerunner stands.

Historical problems are not the most pressing for those caught up in renewal. Controversies about the virgin birth and the empty tomb may be a waste of time. 'It was not the Christ the Virgin Mary carried in her womb who saved us, but the Christ she carried in her heart.' Ronald Knox is right when he says, 'Perhaps the leading characteristic of seventeenth-century English enthusiasm was the distinction ... between the Christ of history and the Christ of experience.'[5]

(3) *Outward Manifestations*

Glossolalia is not always a feature of renewal movements as it has been in Pentecostalism, not least in our own time. It has never been much evident in Methodism. Nor has there been any consistent sign of supernatural phenomena, even though healing ministries are often part of renewal; but not inevitably, though the longer ending of St Mark (16.9ff) does correspond to some Christian experience all over the world. Renewal is, however, accompanied by liveliness – shouting, singing, dancing. Billy Bray, the nineteenth-century Cornish preacher of the Bible Christians, was a converted drunkard, and as eccentric as only a professional comedian can afford to be these days. He danced along the lanes because he was too happy to walk, danced in public with those about whose spiritual state he was satisfied, and laid down and rolled on the ground for joy when he was convinced that his vicar had been evangelically converted.

(4) *Lyricism*

Renewal certainly prompts what Gordon Rupp has called 'a devotion of rapture'.[6] This is evidenced in hymns, which must be distinguished from the formal traditional hymns belonging to the Divine Office and sung to plainsong. The hymns of renewal were often set to popular tunes, like Charles Wesley's 'Love divine, all loves excelling' to Purcell. But perhaps the greatest effect of the

Wesley hymns is that they gave expression to ecstasy but also contained it in poetic forms. They also had the remarkable power of making converted collier drunkards, the riff-raff of society, sing impeccably orthodox Christian doctrine, the mysteries of incarnation and redemption, and the triumph of God's love in the soul leading to perfection.

(5) *Itinerancy*

There is a certain restlessness about leaders and preachers of renewal. Sometimes in the times of Catholic hegemony, when the Church persecuted them, companies of the sects had to wander from place to place. Under Charles II and the Clarendon Code in England, Dissenting congregations took refuge in the Chiltern Hills and sought the cover of Epping Forest. But John Wesley's famous words in answer to those who sought to confine him to preach within parishes by permission of the incumbent, 'I look upon the whole world as my parish', could be the watchword of many leaders of renewal. On the American frontier in the nineteenth-century, the Christian mission was undertaken by the circuit riders travelling from camp to camp. As has been said, the Bishop followed in the train. It was the unordered missioners who offered Christ without the impedimenta of the hierarchy. Jonathan Edwards of the Great Awakening in eighteenth-century America, which preceded by a few years the Methodist Revival, was an exception to this rule. But Howel Harris, for instance, deplored orthodox Dissent, though it had become somewhat aridly intellectual and unitarian by his time, because he felt that the congregational system led to established and settled congregations which so often became prosperous and lost their evangelical zeal. He said of George Whitefield, comparing him to their disadvantage with the Dissenters, 'While they are in their warm rooms, he ventures his life for God.'

(6) *A Crossing of the Sex Barriers*

Women are often prominent in renewal movements, from Maximilla the Montanist onwards. Mysticism has often been the consequence of the rapture of renewal, and there have been many women mystics, notably, in Ronald Knox's treatment of the subject, Madame Guyon. The leaders have often been susceptible to women. This is all part of their inevitably passionate natures and longing for the love of God. John Wesley was notorious in his love affairs, though that is perhaps not the best description of them, since he was ever honourable. His problem was – and it has been argued that this was all of Divine Providence – that he could not bring them to decision. But his susceptibility did not end with his evangelical conversion in 1738. He was always in danger, and the object of scandalous rumour until he married a widow whose total incompatibility meant that he was freed from female adulation and blissful domesticity to continue his itinerant mission. But there has always been in renewal movements an ease of relationship between the sexes which, in spite of perils, does betoken something more natural and more healthy and more helpful than the stilted formalism of courts or of much society before our own time. Some friendships outside marriage were of undoubted inspiration and comfort. The fact that they did not involve lifelong vows, or indeed any vows at all except those of Church membership, may have been a very great advantage to the work of renewal. But there were dangers, not least of gossip, as happened to Agnes Beaumont and John Bunyan, when he took her by pillion to the Lord's Supper in Gamlingay, and her father locked her out on her return.

(7) *Ethical Rigorism*

In spite of relaxing sexual relations, immorality and licentiousness were much deplored in renewal movements, and often there was an austerity which could seem terrifying. The Montanists sought to out-fast and out-discipline the Catholic Church. Remarriage was considered to be adulterous. They were harsh indeed towards human weakness. It was so with some of the Mediaeval sects, such as the Manichees. The Cathari, literally Puritans – herein lies the sting of the name as applied to English Protestants of the sixteenth-century – may have been in danger of seeming to be 'holier than thou'. Avoidance of luxury and plainness of dress came to characterise Quakers, though Margaret Fell, George Fox's wife, opposed it, while Wesley toyed at one time with a uniform for Methodists. It is sad to read of John Pawson, one of Wesley's preachers, destroying, after the latter's death, his copy of Shakespeare with all his copious notes, and also one is grieved at Elizabeth Fry's fear to hum to her baby lest she instilled into him a love of music. This is very different from the original Quaker singing, and indeed music was the one art of which the Puritans approved, and which in general has found place in renewal. As readers of Nathaniel Hawthorne's *The Scarlet Letter* know well, the ethical rigorism of second generation renewalists often engendered resentment and rebellion; but this is a strain which counterparts the lyricism and the freedom of expression.

(8) *Ecumenism*

This may be contrary to what is popularly supposed, and the ecumenism of renewal movements is very different from that which has dominated the debates of the traditional Churches in our own century. In fact, renewal is not particularly interested in questions of faith and order, nor in the divisions which differences about them have created. John Wesley loved holiness wherever he found it. His *Christian Library,* in fifty volumes, includes extracts not only from the Fathers but from the English Puritans and also from such Catholic and Counter-Reformation sources as he knew. Anyone whose life was filled with God, whatever his century or allegiance, was for him an example to be studied and followed. His sermon on 'Catholic Spirit', following William Law, was on 2 Kings 10.15, 'Is thy heart right, as my heart is with thy heart? ... If it be, give me thine hand'.

(9) *Politics*

Renewal movements which transcended categories of orthodox thought were always under suspicion in case they sought to undermine the state. There is no doubt that because they appealed to the poor and made them articulate, they did have political ramifications, as Christopher Hill has shown in many of his studies of the Puritan underworld in the seventeenth century. If, of course, you feel that the religious element in renewal is bound to disappear with advancing knowledge and civilisation, then there is only politics left. But it must not be forgotten that the Primitive Methodists had great influence in the formation of trade unions, which were modelled on the Methodist societies. The Tolpuddle Martyrs were Primitive Methodists; but the heavenly dimension was never lost, and renewal always offered a salvation beyond this world, even though it inspired men and women to work for better conditions. The confidence with which they were able to oppose tyrants, if not to subdue kingdoms, was born of their assurance of their standing before God, and of their heavenly inheritance.

THE DANGERS

We have already hinted that these movements might in some ways run amok. The Montanists in the beginnings of church history did not scruple to believe that, possessed by the Spirit, they were themselves divine. Maximilla said 'I am the Word and the Spirit and Power'; also 'I am the lyre and the Spirit is the plectrum'. Montanus declared 'I am the Father, the Word and the Paraclete'. There is in the seventeenth century the tragic story of James Nayler, who one dreadful day entered Bristol on horseback surrounded by adoring followers who cried 'Blessed is he who comes in the name of the Lord'. The recovery of Nayler from this blasphemy, and the bitter tortures which followed, is one of the most moving stories of church history, for he came to understand that possession by the Spirit of Christ is something which must be evidenced, not in such extravagances but in humble love.

There is also the danger of lack of proportion, of exaggerating truths, of what has been called 'Jesusism', in which a sentimental, erotic devotion to Jesus has replaced the love of the Father to whom he leads us. Pentecostalism may concentrate too much upon the Holy Spirit, and not understand that the Spirit is given only through the sufferings and glorification of Christ.

Renewal sometimes may be vulgar. It also may embarrass those whose temperament does not make them yield to it, who, like the Tractarians, are persuaded of the doctrine of reserve and who, with them and with Dietrich Bonhoeffer in our own time, believe that Christian discipline is arcane, hidden from the world, and that the mysteries of the Gospel are not to be blurted out at every street corner. Isaac Williams, the Tractarian poet, complained of evangelical preaching of the atonement that this 'the highest and most sacred of all Christian doctrines, is to be pressed before and pressed home to all persons indiscriminately, and most especially to those who are living unchristian lives'. He went on to say that Paul's preaching of Christ crucified means 'the necessity of our being crucified to the world', not shouting about the blood to all and sundry. Bad taste may not be numbered among the deadly sins, and yet there are some deplorable examples, even in the preaching of such as Whitefield. John Wesley talked of 'the old coarse Gospel', and he is right against the precious and snobbish and the squeamish aristocrats of his day. Calvary was no scene of aesthetic beauty. And yet reverence is a virtue, not least before the impenetrable mystery of 'God made man for man to die'. Nor should we be too familiar with holy things, and make the high God our own possession, one whom we may tame and domesticate, of whose mysterious ways we are absolutely sure.[7]

There is also a danger of anti-intellectualism. Although, as is so often being said these days, we do not enter the kingdom of heaven simply by ratiocination, and we may have made the Gospel too academic, we do need light as well as warmth, and unless there is a spirit of criticism within the Christian fellowship, we may find that we are failing to discern the spirits. This has been a danger of renewal movements, and led them sometimes to violence and atrocities.

There are also ugly stories of contention, of schism. It is sad indeed that Methodism, whose 'grand depositum', in the words of its founder, was to preach scriptural holiness and the hope of perfect love, should, in the nineteenth century, have been rent asunder by such squalid strife and a nastiness which makes one ashamed. Yet perhaps in the end Baxter is right: 'It is better that men should be disorderly saved than orderly damned, and that the Church should be disorderly preserved than orderly destroyed.' Something of the life of Christ and the Divine Spirit has been revealed and bestowed through movements which have reacted against the tidiness and the orthodoxy of the great Church.

The worst danger in any study of renewal movements is nostalgia for the past. It is contrary to the very spirit of renewal to be looking back and to say 'Lord, do it again'. Renewal is a better term than revival, because revival has the connotation of seeking to bring about the past again, whereas God is always preparing to do a new thing. Revivalism, too, may fail to read the signs of our different times. The study of the history of renewal is valuable and important because history teaches proportion and warns against dangers; though it also should mark the end of 'old unhappy far-off things and battles long ago'. As Eliot says, those who were divided in the past are now 'enfolded in a single party', and we may honour their sanctity while remembering that they, too, were not already made perfect.

One longs that the ecumenism of our time may bring renewal. It has so far failed to do so, though through a sharing of traditions and an increase in charity there has been a renewal of some kind, which may be the beginning. The way forward is through sharing of experience, an ability to learn from all, even those traditions most alien to us, and a patient waiting upon God, who, as John

Robinson, the Pilgrim Father, said in often quoted words, 'has yet more truth and light to break forth from his holy Word'. But renewal cannot be planned; or even attained by faith and prayer. Cecil Day Lewis has a poem 'Final Instructions' in which an old priest of an unnamed cult talks to a novice about the ritual of Sacrifice:

> The celebrant's approach may be summed up
> In three words – patience, joy,
> Disinterestedness
>
> But the crucial point is this:
> You are called only to *make* the sacrifice:
> Whether or not he enters into it
> Is the god's affair; and whatever the handbooks say,
> You can neither command his presence nor explain it –
> All you can do is to make it possible.
> If the sacrifice catches fire of its own accord
> On the altar, well and good. But do not
> Flatter yourself that discipline and devotion
> Have wrought the miracle: they have only allowed it.

NOTES

[1] J. H. Newman, *An Essay on the Development of Christian Doctrine,* new ed, Longmans, Green and Co., 1885, p. 40. The Essay was first published in 1845.

[2] Geoffrey F. Nuttall, *The Puritan Spirit,* Epworth Press 1976, p. 172.

[3] Charles Wesley, *Journal,* ed. Thomas Jackson (1849) i. 226-7, quoted by Geoffrey F. Nuttall, *Howel Harris (1714-1773), The Last Enthusiast,* University of Wales Press 1965, pp. 54-5, a work to which I am greatly indebted.

[4] Nuttall, ibid., pp. 55-6.

[5] R. A. Knox, *Enthusiasm,* OUP 1950, p. 175.

[6] Gordon Rupp, 'A Devotion of Rapture in English Puritanism', in R. Buick Knox, ed., *Reformation, Conformity and Dissent: Essays in Honour of Geoffrey Nuttall,* pp. 115-131.

[7] This sense of the mystery of God is well brought out in Nicholas Lash, *Theology on the Road to Emmaus,* SCM Press 1986, particularly in Chapter 1.

12

Walking in the Spirit: Freedom and Tradition in the Church's Life

A. M. Allchin

It is characteristic of the work of the Holy Spirit that he enables us to see new things and to see old things in new ways. Sometimes these discoveries are absurdly simple, yet potentially profound. Such a discovery came to me while listening some years ago to Cardinal Suenens, surely one of the outstanding figures in the movement of renewal, not only in the Roman Catholic Church but far beyond. Speaking of the need for both continuity and change in the Church, the Cardinal used the simplest of images. To walk, he said, you need to have one foot off the ground, in movement, and one foot on the ground, not in movement. It won't do to have both on or both off the ground at the same time!

The statement, for all its simplicity, has innumerable implications. Growth in an institution as well as in an individual implies both continuity and change. Tradition involves not only respect for the past but anticipation of the future. The political oppositions between conservative and progressive, which the media are always trying to impose on us, are meaningless and positively harmful when applied to the life of the Church, which must always unite within itself a profound memory of what God has done in the past with an unlimited hope for what God will do in the future. As S. T. Coleridge said, 'Without memory there can be no hope'. It is indeed precisely the work of God the Holy Spirit to overcome the destructive oppositions which can arrive in the life of the Church and the life of its members, oppositions of head and heart, of authority and freedom, of corporate and personal, no less than of care for the past and anticipation of the future. The Holy Spirit is the one who binds the Church into one, and at the same time gives different gifts to each of its members, he is the source at once of its unity and diversity. It is he who recalls to us the deeds of God in the history of his people and at the same time opens our hearts and minds to the reality of the Kingdom which is still to come

THE RECONCILIATION OF HEART AND MIND

To understand the nature of the tradition, and the work of the Holy Spirit as the constant source of new life within that tradition, we need to indulge in 'polarity thinking', a way of thinking which enables us to hold together apparent opposites, which refuses to accept the divisions which the fallen world tries to put upon us. This is a way of thinking and seeing and acting which opens our hearts and minds to the paradoxes of the faith, to the unity of the three persons in the one Godhead, to the unity of the two natures, human and divine, in the person of the incarnate Word, to the coming together of divine authority and human freedom in the free obedience of our response to the call of God.[1] It is the Holy Spirit who holds together many things, inner and outer, subjective and objective, personal and corporate, human and divine, in the reconciling action of his love.

These are not just abstract generalisations. They work out in practice when people begin to be aware of the action of the Holy Spirit in their lives. I think for instance of a parish where a number of people find that they are weeping when they pray and are troubled at such an un-English phenomenon, until they find that the gift of tears has an honourable place in the history of Christian prayer and faith. They are rediscovering an element of Christian and human experience which our age has largely inhibited, which we greatly need if we are to rediscover the power and meaning of such words as repentance, compassion and hope. I think again of someone who came to see me recently to say how much it had meant to her to discover the writings of Symeon the New Theologian. The eleventh-century Byzantine abbot, until recently considered the preserve of specialists in patristic studies, had spoken to her directly of her own experience of the work of the Holy Spirit, had illuminated and confirmed things which she had tentatively begun to acknowledge in herself. It is as though God the Holy Spirit was bringing to our minds things hidden in the tradition which even a short while ago would have seemed to us irrelevant and remote.

A very striking and more public example of this phenomenon is to be seen in Britain and elsewhere, in the concern for the writings of the fourteenth-century English mystics, in all their richness and diversity: Richard Rolle with his heartfelt, charismatic devotion, full of fire and song, the author of *The Cloud of Unknowing* with his insistent call to us to go beyond words in our approach to God, Julian of Norwich with her hardly won assurance that in the end all manner of things shall be well. These are books which are read not simply as texts from the past, but as sources of light and insight for today. They suggest to us very forcibly that contemporary movements of spiritual renewal are more closely linked with one another and with their common past than we might at first sight imagine. Movements of prayer which are exuberant and expressive, movements of prayer which are quiet and contemplative, have it in common that they both bring men and women to the point where they discover that prayer is not primarily something that we *do*. Prayer is a gift; prayer is God himself praying in us.

Where the Holy Spirit is at work in the Church, he brings both renewal of what is old, and also new light and new understanding, challenging not only our sluggish hearts and wills but also the lazy habits of our minds, stimulating us to new and creative thinking. If there has been a failure in the movements of renewal which have been taking place in our Churches in the last twenty-five years, and in the Church's response to them, it has often been, I believe, at this point of *thought*. We have not thought enough about what God is saying to us through them, we have not given enough attention either to the way in which what is happening now relates to what has happened in earlier centuries or to the way in which movements of the Spirit within the Church relate to movements of the Spirit in the world around us. We have recognised our need to rethink our theology of the Holy Spirit and our understanding of Christian spirituality, but as yet we have only made a beginning in these things.

Too often it has happened that those immediately involved in various aspects of renewal have allowed themselves to become suspicious of probing intellectual questions, trapped into narrow and inadequate ways of thinking about their experience. Frequently, for instance, the identification of a particular experience in prayer, 'tongue-speaking', with 'baptism in the Spirit' has had the result of dividing congregations into what are felt to be first and second class Christians, and has put an undue weight on one particular experience of God's grace, as if it in itself were determinative of his favour. On the other hand those involved in academic theology have too often allowed their entrenched habits of mind, their unease with certain manifestations of enthusiasm, to prevent them entering sympathetically into the reality of these movements. They have failed to see their healing potential, their capacity to challenge the rigidities of 'fundamentalism' no less than the rigidities of academic 'liberalism'. As Stephen Parsons points out in a recent study of the phenomena of Christian healing, these particular movements, in their vitality and diversity, question the certainties both of scientific medicine and of our post-enlightenment rational theology, but they also demand for their interpretation a viewpoint much wider and more inclusive than that of biblical fundamentalism.[2] We need a way of understanding which will break through the narrowness of our specialisations, medical and psychological, theological and spiritual. If the Holy Spirit brings healing to the *whole* of our human nature, then surely we need a *whole* way of approach to the understanding of his action. We need the convergence of many viewpoints, many disciplines, to the understanding of this fullness of God's grace.

LIBERATION THROUGH THE LITURGY

The willingness to make use of convergent methods of approach to questions, the recognition that God speaks to us not in one but in many ways, has been a characteristic of Anglicanism since the Reformation. Scripture, tradition, right reason are all necessary in the Church's life; sometimes we need to emphasise one, sometimes another element in the triad. And undoubtedly this tradition continues to exercise a powerful attraction, precisely on account of its balanced and many-sided quality, being at once biblical in its foundations, yet open to learn from the long history of Christian East and West, open to learn too from the findings of the human sciences today. It is instructive for those of us who are Anglicans by birth to discover what it is in our way of life which speaks most powerfully to Christians of other traditions and draws them into the Anglican family. We have here a remarkable testimony in a book of essays published last year in the United States of America, called *Evangelicals on the Canterbury Trail*.[3] It is a book which contains the stories of a number of men and women who have found their way into the Episcopal Church, and who, without in any way wishing to repudiate their evangelical origins, have discovered there a catholicity of faith and life which has been for them healing and life-giving. It is a book which brings us into contact with the huge and burgeoning world of conservative evangelicalism, particularly strong in the mid-west and south-west of the United States, and enables us to see ourselves from an unfamiliar viewpoint. In its pages we find a search for a holistic spirituality and a balanced understanding of the Christian way of prayer and faith. This is a spirituality which can integrate commitment, enthusiasm, feeling into a larger and more inclusive whole, a spirituality which will touch body as well as soul, which will engage us in our social as well as in our personal existence, which will respect our intellectual and aesthetic capacities and which will be open to receive from all the major traditions which have marked the Christian centuries. It is the possibility of such a spirituality which has attracted men and women to the Episcopal Church at a time when its public image has at times been obscured by controversy and dissensions. It is a possibility which for them has been conveyed through the Church's liturgy as they have found it celebrated in ordinary American parishes, in the forms provided by the Book of Common Prayer of 1979.

In the liturgy we find a way of prayer which by being wholly centred on God is able to unite apparent opposites. It is at once biblical and catholic, traditional yet contemporary, personal and corporate. It provides a way of liberation from the subjectivism and man-centredness of much evangelical worship, which is presented as oscillating between emotionalism on the one side and didacticism on the other. By its very nature the liturgy provides an awareness of history which frees us from the parochialism of the present. It also provides a means by which our feeling and our thinking may be fused together into a total act of adoration. Through the use of symbolic action and bodily gesture, the body itself is caught up into this activity. At its heart there stand the sacraments, life-giving symbols which bring together head and heart, individual and community, past and present, human and divine.

> Liturgical worship allowed me to forget myself in a corporate action not contingent on my own feelings at the moment for its effect. The efficacy of the liturgy does depend on faith, but efficacy resides within the corporate *act,* performed in faith, rather than on the faith as evidenced in

the subjective *feelings* of the individuals present. Participation in liturgical worship frees the self from its own subjective self-consciousness and places him in a 'work of the people', as liturgy means, larger than his own private acts of piety. Invited to experience the ordering shape of the liturgy, I experienced not constriction but liberation. And lo and behold, submission to the liturgy prompted the recovery of personal involvement and pious feelings.[4]

The writer, John Skillen, an associate professor of English in a New England college, is pointing here to a matter of the utmost importance. How is it that we are able to go beyond our own experience of God into the mystery of God himself? How is it that our own small realisation of the presence of God, which may be for us, at times, intensely real and powerful, can become not turned in on itself, but open to the awareness of God's presence with his people through the ages, known in the experience of countless other men and women of many different cultures, types and traditions? It is not just a matter of being at one with a large number of contemporaries. It is something stranger and more mysterious than that, something which touches on the reality which we call the communion of saints. John Skillen asks himself how it was that the liturgy even in a quite small congregation conveyed a sense of catholicity which was lacking even in some very large gatherings and conventions.

> Why, before I gave much thought to catholicity and authority, did I feel more part of a catholic church among two hundred at Christ Church, than among eighteen thousand at Urbana '70? One reason is that true catholicity never has the quality of being staged. Catholicity is not just conjured up; it exists. The church does not create its catholicity; it is obedient to it. I was troubled by feelings of unity and catholicity that appeared to be produced by the emotional immediacy of the event.[5]

The context shows that these remarks are made from the background of a conservative rather than a charismatic evangelicalism. But I believe they would apply as well in a charismatic as in a non-charismatic situation. They tell us about an awareness of catholicity which is deeper than the emotions, of a concern for catholicity in time as well as in space, of a search for a fuller and more balanced apprehension of the faith.

For the editor of the volume, Dr Robert Webber, Professor of Theology at the well-known evangelical college at Wheaton, Illinois, a large part of the appeal of the Church's liturgical tradition has come from the fact that it presents a framework of Christian faith and understanding which is definite and orthodox without being constricting or over-defined. It presents a way out of a literalist understanding of the Bible, a recovery of poetic and symbolic forms of thinking and a liberation from highly structured rationalist theological systems. It opens a way into a sense of the mystery and majesty of God himself, God who goes beyond all our formulations about him. By discarding 'logical systems about God' he found himself free to enter into a deeper encounter with God himself, 'a mystery that defies a complete explanation, that rises above all rational systems and pat answers'. To enter on this way is to set out on a journey which leads us 'into the mystery of God's saving presence in Christ communicated through worship and the sacraments'.[6]

As has already been stated, *Evangelicals on the Canterbury Trail* is a book which reflects a Calvinistic rather than a charismatic style of evangelical Christianity. But much that is said in its pages about the power of the liturgy to free us from the subjectivity of self-conscious feeling and the parochialism of the present would be true for one who approached the liturgy from a more distinctively charismatic experience of faith and worship. From such a background, however, one would expect the theological emphasis of the book to be different. In Dr Webber's presentation of the matter it is always the Christological character of the liturgy which is stressed. It is in worship, through the sacraments, that we are made partakers of Christ's incarnation, death and resurrection. All this is finely stated. But it is striking that almost nothing is said about the role of the Holy Spirit in the Church's worship, about the Eucharist as the constant presence of Pentecost in the Church. The discovery that Sunday is a weekly renewal of Pentecost, as well as of Easter, is surely one of the great gifts of God to the Church in the last quarter of a century.

THE INVOCATION OF THE HOLY SPIRIT

The discovery that the Church's life and worship is essentially *epicletic,* i.e. centred on the invocation of the Holy Spirit, is one of the primary factors which in this generation has brought the Western Churches, Catholic and Protestant, much closer to one another and to the world of Eastern Orthodoxy. This is a remarkable fact, and one that has been too little noticed. It is striking how strong the emphasis is on the role of the Holy Spirit in the Eucharist in the BEM documents, for instance. In the new Eucharistic prayers to be found in the Anglican liturgies, the Trinitarian nature of the prayer is always made explicit in a way in which it was not either in 1552 or 1662. It is in the power of the Spirit that Christ comes to meet us in the sacrament of his body and blood. It is in the power of the Spirit that the Church's offering is made one with Christ's own offering. Through Christ we approach the Father, in the power of the Spirit. This rediscovery of the role of the Holy Spirit in the Eucharist has been part of a large movement of thought, an opening out into a new yet ancient understanding of the Holy Spirit's role in the whole life and faith and worship of the Church. At this point the work of the Anglican – Orthodox Joint Doctrinal Commission has a particular contribution to make, since the Orthodox have always maintained a strong emphasis on the work of the Holy Spirit in the whole of the Church's sacramental life. There is material here which would be relevant and useful far beyond the realm of those directly concerned in relations with the Orthodox Churches.[7]

When we turn to the texts of the two agreed statements, of Moscow 1979 and Dublin 1984, we find that they are constantly concerned to link together personal and corporate in the Church's faith and prayer, and to see the Church's inner life in sacrament and worship in indissoluble relationship with its outer life of service and mission to the world.

> Witness, evangelism, service, worship and sacrifice belong together, for these are different sides of the same reality ... Worship involves service of the people (its ancient meaning) when we worship Christ by ministering to him in the sick, the prisoners and the needy. (Matt. 25.37-40) Where the Church is not at liberty to organise developed social and philanthropic programmes of its own or to take part in those organised jointly with others, its witness is carried out through worship, prayer and personal ministry. The Church can bear witness not only in word and deed but also in silence. (DAS 33)

This silent witness may sometimes take the ultimate form of martyrdom, witness unto death. This is a fact which our talkative busy Churches in Western Europe and North America need to remember. It is a part of the living experience of Churches living under totalitarian regimes whether in Eastern Europe, in Central and South America, or in other parts of the Third World.

But all this activity is carried on in the power of the Spirit. For it is by the invocation of the Spirit that the Church lives in every aspect of its being.

> Although epiclesis (invocation of the Spirit) has a special meaning in the Eucharist, we must not restrict the concept to the Eucharist alone. In every sacrament, prayer and blessing, the Church invokes the Holy Spirit, and in all these various ways calls upon him to sanctify the whole creation. The Church is that community which lives by continually invoking the Holy Spirit. (MAS 32)

The whole creation is touched by the Spirit's love, since in all things the Holy Spirit is at work, as Lord and Life-giver. This universal action of God in all creation is the necessary presupposition for the special presence of the Spirit in the Church, God's new dwelling place in our midst. It is in the coming of the Holy Spirit at Pentecost that the Church is founded, and it is the action of the Holy Spirit in the heart of each believer which forms the deepest reality of our prayer. Prayer is nothing less than God himself in us. It is when we know that we have been taken beyond ourselves, whether into the silence of adoration or the exuberance of praise, that we know for a moment the wonder of this affirmation.

'Although prayer is at one level a human activity, at a deeper level it is the activity in us of God the Holy Spirit who dwells in our hearts by faith' (DAS 38; cf. Rom. 8.26-29). 'Common to East and West alike is the experience of the Holy Spirit praying in us, of which St Paul speaks in Galatians 4.5-7, "God has sent the Spirit of his Son into our hearts, crying, Abba, Father"' (DAS 39). 'The Holy Spirit praying in us heals and restores us at the centre of our being, that is to say in our hearts' (DAS 37). This concept of the heart as the centre of our being is of vital importance. It is the place where our different faculties are to be fused into one; the focal point of understanding, thought and memory, intuition, love and longing, the deep centre of personal existence, full of words but still more full of a silence which goes beyond words. It is here that the Holy Spirit dwells, 'cleansing the thoughts of our hearts', so that we can grow into the perfection of God's love and come to magnify his name in a way which befits his infinite glory. This action of the Spirit, though it is usually secret and hidden, often unknown to the one in whom it takes place, yet has consequences in the world around us. As St Seraphim of Sarov (d.1833) said, 'Have peace in your heart and thousands around you will find God's peace', so the Commission affirms in less eloquent terms, 'The healing character of the grace of the Holy Trinity in the life of the individual believer and of the Church has important implications for the whole life of contemporary society' (DAS 37).

This healing power of the Holy Spirit can be seen at work in the lives of individuals in a variety of ways, sometimes in the form of physical healing, sometimes in the healing of memories, sometimes in liberation from old fears and inhibitions. It can be seen in the life of the Christian community, as it is drawn together into the communion of the Holy Spirit. It is at the heart of the movement towards unity. Here is another vital meaning of the invocation of the Holy Spirit in the Eucharist.

> The unity of the members of the Church is renewed by the Spirit in the Eucharistic act. The Spirit comes not only upon the elements, but on the community. The Epiclesis is a double invocation; by the invocation of the Spirit the members of Christ are fed with his Body and Blood so that they may grow in holiness and may be strong to manifest Christ to the world and to do his work in the power of the Spirit. (MAS 31)

The Church is in no way a society which exists for itself. It exists for God, it exists for God's world. Its life is caught up into the very life of the Tri-une God, the God whose care and love extends to all creation.

> The Eucharist impels the believers to specific action in mission and service to the world. In the Eucharistic celebration the Church is a confessing community which witnesses to the cosmic transfiguration. (MAS 28).

TIME TRANSFIGURED

Many of the themes which are present in the tradition of the Church's worship find expression in these texts, above all the sense that the whole creation, 'everything that has breath', is to be caught up into the praise of God through the worship of the Church. We can gain here a glimpse of what would be involved in the renewal of the Church's worship and in the renewal of the Church itself, gathered together in the power of the Spirit, the community assembling and distributing the many and varied gifts which God has given to men and women, enabling us to share together the resources of creation for the benefit of all, and allowing us to transfigure the complexity of the world which God has made, so that all things become transparent to the operations of God's wisdom and God's love, so that we may see the truth of what we proclaim day by day, 'heaven and earth are full of thy glory'.

But all this in its diversity and multiplicity is centred in the person and work of Christ the Redeemer made known to us in the coming of the Comforter.

> In the coming of the Paraclete, the whole mystery of Christ is realised; the Holy Spirit takes the things of Christ and shows them to us, making them real in every age; the Paraclete is thus the constant source of life in the tradition of the Church. (DAS 59)

Here is another way in which the Spirit brings things into unity. For tradition here is not seen simply as the conservation and handing on of a deposit from the past, but as a dynamic force constantly renewed and energised by the ferment of the Creator Spirit. This is the spring of life welling up into eternal life in the heart of the Church and the heart of each believer. In it past and present are reconciled, death is overcome, the generations meet together in the communion of saints.

> The Church in the celebration of its liturgy recalls the mighty acts of God in the past, experiences them as present and living realities, and anticipates the coming of the Lord in glory. In the presence of the risen Christ we receive the promise of the coming Kingdom. Liturgical time is no cold and lifeless represention of past events, nor simply an historical record. It is Christ himself living in the Church. Liturgical time is time transfigured through liturgical act, for it is time animated by 'the fervour of faith, full of the Holy Spirit. (DAS 56)

The last words are those which the priest says in the Liturgy of St John Chrysostom when immediately before the moment of communion he adds a little hot water to what is in the chalice. Whatever the historical origin of this gesture may have been, in its present form it speaks eloquently of the presence of pentecostal fire, personal fervour at the heart of the Church's worship. It helps us to understand what might be meant by the transfiguration of time, not only in the sense that charismatic acts of worship, like those of the Orthodox tradition, often go on for a very long time and do not feel constrained by the clock, but also in the profounder sense that in the immediacy of the divine presence time is experienced not so much as the spreading out of one event after another, but rather as their being gathered together into a moment of fullness, into the fullness of time. This is a moment in which past and future are reconciled and at one in the presence of eternity, a moment in which death is overcome in the power of God's love, in the power of the one who is God not of the dead but of the living, for all live to him. In such a time we taste the reality of the Kingdom which is to come.

> Our experience of the communion of saints finds its fullest expression in the Eucharist in which the whole body of Christ realises its unity in the Holy Spirit ... Union with God therefore involves us in a personal relationship with all who belong to him through the grace of the Holy Spirit who both unites and diversifies; and this personal relationship which is not broken by death is precisely the communion of saints. (DAS 68, 69)

We worship with angels and archangels and with all the company of heaven.

If we are to walk, we shall need to have one foot on the ground and one off it. We shall need the virtues of discernment and discretion, no less than of commitment and enthusiasm. We shall need to be willing to learn from many and unexpected sources past and present, for the Holy Spirit is Lord and Life-giver and is bounded by none of our definitions. Above all we shall need to live more truly in the power which comes from him, acknowledging at every moment that 'the Church is that community which lives by continually invoking the Holy Spirit'.

NOTES

[1] For a discussion of 'polarity thinking' in one particular but highly influential thinker see Owen Barfield's book, *What Coleridge Thought* (1971) and specially chapter 12, 'Man and God', pp. 144-157.

[2] Stephen Parsons, *The Challenge of Christian Healing* (1986, in particular chapter 9, 'Towards a Theology of Healing – Holistic Theology', pp. 148 ff.

[3] *Evangelicals on the Canterbury Trail: Why Evangelicals are Attracted to the Liturgical Church,* ed. Robert E. Webber, Word Books, Waco, Texas, 1985.

[4] Ibid., p. 128.

[5] Ibid., p. 128.

[6] Ibid., p. 30.

[7] The texts of the two agreed statements, Moscow 1976 and Dublin 1984, are published in the booklet *Anglican-Orthodox Dialogue,* SPCK 1984. References are given in the text to the paragraphs in the two statements, i.e. MAS and DAS.